THE TOP ON~~E~~

ITALIAN RI~~CE DISHES~~

Also by Diane Seed

THE TOP ONE HUNDRED PASTA SAUCES
EATING OUT IN ITALY
FAVORITE INDIAN FOOD
THE TOP 100 ITALIAN DISHES
DIANE SEED'S TOP 100 MEDITERRANEAN DISHES
DIANE SEED'S ROME FOR ALL SEASONS

Diane Seed, internationally renowned cookbook author and food writer, runs a cooking school in the heart of Rome and can be contacted there by fax (+39 06 679 7109) or e-mail (dianeseed@compuserve.com)

DIANE SEED

THE TOP ONE HUNDRED ITALIAN RICE DISHES

Including over 50 Risotto Recipes

Illustrations by Sarah Hocombe

Ten Speed Press
Berkeley / Toronto

**To Alex, Max, Christopher and Jamie,
and Jezzy and Tasha, who kept me company all through
the long, hot Rome summer.**

A Kirsty Melville Book

1☉

Ten Speed Press
P.O. Box 7123
Berkeley, California 94707
www.tenspeed.com

Distributed in Canada by Ten Speed Press Canada.

Library of Congress Cataloging-in-Publication Data is on file with the publisher.

ISBN 1-58008-280-7

First USA printing, 2000
Printed in Italy

1 2 3 4 5 6 7 8 9 10 — 04 03 02 01 00

CONTENTS

INTRODUCTION

THE HISTORY OF RICE IN ITALY

Many years ago, when I was researching the history of pasta, I became bewildered by conflicting stories of Marco Polo, the ancient Romans and even Lucrezia Borgia! The story of rice is equally confused, but most people believe that it was brought to Sicily by the Arabs in the eighth or ninth century. These early rice dishes, which were baked or fried, did not have an influence on other neighboring regions until the Spanish *Aragonesi* took them to Puglia and Campania in the thirteenth and fourteenth centuries. Botanical gardens experimented and soon the monasteries discovered the benefits of this economical crop. By the fifteenth century we find the Benedictine monks at Montecassino carefully selecting the best of the available seeds and starting extensive cultivation. In the north, soon to become the center of Italian rice cultivation, we can find probably the first mention of rice in the early fourteenth century in the household accounts of Torino's Duke of Savoia, and it is recorded in 1475 that Milan's ruling Sforza family sent twelve sacks of seeds to the Duke of Ferrara.

Rice cultivation needs flat land and access to a lot of water so the area around the river Po proved ideal. Milan was the first area in the north to use rice as a complete dish rather than just as a boiled cereal in soups. It is thought that the word risotto came from Lombardian dialect to describe a more compact rice dish. After Milan came Vercelli, Novara and Lomellina, and in 1874 the Cavour canal was opened in Piemonte providing the largest area of rice fields, 573 acres.

Mantova and the area around Venice are also important rice producers and, in 1644, the Venetian Republic granted permission to establish a mill in Isola della Scala near Venice.

Cultivating rice was very labor-intensive in the spring when the land had to be dug over and fertilized after the hard northern winter. The seeds had to be soaked in water before planting so that they started to germinate before being sown and the rice fields had to be flooded with water from the canals so that the seedlings would be protected from the sharp drop in temperature during the night. However, the real back-breaking work was the weeding. In May the rice fields had to be weeded to prevent the young rice from being choked by other vegetation. Hundreds of women known as *le mondine*, or weeders, arrived from all parts of Italy to perform the delicate task of rooting out the weeds while leaving the young rice in place.

Le mondine have become a nostalgic memory, immortalized by the famous film *Riso Amaro*, or 'Bitter Rice', featuring a young Silvana Mangano. It was a hard life for *le modine*, living together in dormitories housing hundreds of women far from their homes. They had to work bent double, up to their knees in water under a blazing sun. They were bitten by mosquitoes and the water teemed with wildlife. They worked in rows, moving backwards, controlled by an overseer who sat high on a chair like a tennis umpire. When the women approached the end of a field the overseer called out for the central girls to move out in order to leave a space for the frogs (which had been driven back as they progressed down the field) to escape. It is said that the water seemed to boil as all the wildlife made a mass exit. As the women weeded they sang. One of the songs, '*Ciao Bella*', was adopted by the Italian Communist Party to express the social injustice of the system.

Le mondine and their songs have disappeared and modern machinery makes rice cultivation much easier. Today the rice fields seem an oasis of tranquillity with their shining waters mirroring the lines of the poplar trees.

ITALIAN RICE

Today Italy is the major European rice producer, exporting about 60 percent of what is produced. Most Italian regions have at least one traditional rice dish but in Piemonte, Lombardia and the Veneto rice is more important than pasta. This tradition has probably evolved because when the weather is icy and the chill winds swirl around, penetrating everywhere, a plate of rice gives instant comfort and retains its heat much longer than a plate of pasta.

Italian law requires rice to be divided into six different categories: *Comuni*, *Semifini*, *Fini*, *Superfini*, *Parboiled* and *Integrale*. Each type of rice fits into one of these categories but it is confusing because the same rice can appear in conflicting categories due to regional differences. In practice many of these rices are unavailable outside the area where they are produced and often the choice is limited.

Although experts generally choose a different rice for *minestre*, *antipasti*, risotto, baked rice and *dolci*, in most cases the choice is limited to Carnaroli, Vialone Nano and Arborio. Carnaroli is most popular in Piemonte and Lombardia, while Vialone

Nano is the preferred rice around Mantova, Verona and Venice.

In each recipe I have suggested appropriate types of rice in order of preference based on the region of origin and the type of dish. In this collection there are no recipes designed for parboiled, precooked or brown rice. These are not used in traditional Italian cooking and are not suitable for making any risotto.

How to Cook Rice

In Italian cooking it is very important that the rice should never be washed. Any discolored grains that have escaped the factory detector can be removed but washing damages the grains and reduces the starch needed for a successful Italian rice dish.

Risotto

To make a successful risotto it is important to use the right pan. The pan should be wide and not too deep, with a large, heavy bottom made of a material that is a good conductor of heat so that the rice cooks evenly.

The best rice to use for risotto is Carnaroli or Vialone Nano. Arborio can be used if these are not available but the resulting texture is usually less creamy. The usual amount to cook is between 50g/2 oz (⅓ cup) to 100g/4 oz (⅔ cup) per person, depending on how rich the other ingredients are, and appetites of course!

It is essential to have a pan of boiling stock or water simmering at the side of the risotto pan: 400g/14 oz (2⅓ cups) of rice usually requires 1.5 litres/2¾ pints (6 cups) of liquid but extra boiling water should always be available. If you are making a stock from some of the recipe ingredients, as is the case with *Risotto con Asparagi* (see page 9), add less water to the original stock and then add boiling water as necessary. This avoids wasting some of the precious asparagus flavor.

Method

Heat the butter or olive oil in the pan and gently cook the finely chopped onion until soft. It should not be allowed to change color.

Add the rice and stir it gently around the pan for several minutes to coat the grains in the butter or oil. A flat wooden spoon is the ideal implement since metal tends to damage the grains. The Italians use the term 'toasting' for this process but it is misleading because the rice must not change color.

White wine is sometimes added at this stage and allowed to evaporate before beginning the important process of gradually adding boiling liquid.

Stir in the boiling stock or water a ladle at a time. The rice must be allowed to absorb the liquid before more is added because it should never be drowned. It must be stirred continuously during this process. The rice keeps absorbing liquid until it is three times its original weight. It will take between 15 to 20 minutes to cook properly – until it is *al dente*, which means there should be no gritty texture in the center of the grain but the rice should still offer a slight resistance or bite. At this stage the risotto is shiny and opaque.

Traditionally, cheese is not served with fish dishes. However, in other risottos the final stage usually involves adding butter and freshly grated Parmesan to the rice. Take the pan off the heat and stir vigorously adding the butter (at room temperature) and grated cheese. Cover the pan and allow to rest for 2 minutes. The finished risotto should be creamy due to the released starch.

Risottos from the area around Venice are more liquid and should ripple like a wave when the plate is tilted. This is called *all'onda*.

Boiled Rice

Bring 1.5 litres/2¾ pints (6 cups) of water to a boil in a large saucepan, add a little salt then pour in 400g/14 oz (2⅓ cups) of rice. Leave the pan uncovered and cook over a medium heat, stirring from time to time. The rice usually takes between 12 to 15 minutes to cook. Drain at once and add the rest of the ingredients while the rice is still hot, unless you are making a salad.

How to Deep-fry

In Mediterranean countries there is a long-established tradition of deep-frying. Humble ingredients are deep-fried in olive oil to transform them into crisp, golden morsels of temptation. There is even an old proverb from Liguria that says: *'Fritta é buona persino una scarpa'* – even an old shoe tastes good when it's fried.

When food is fried in olive oil, 60 percent of the moisture content of the food has to evaporate before the oil begins to penetrate, whereas other fats penetrate more deeply into the food. This means food fried in olive oil has a crunchy texture and is less greasy than food fried in other fats.

Six Golden Rules for Deep-frying

1 You must use enough oil to get a satisfactory result. The amount varies according to the pan used for frying. If using an electric fryer follow the maker's directions. If using an ordinary pan you need a minimum depth of 2 inches. Heat the olive oil slowly until it reaches the desired temperature.

2 It is very important to control the temperature of the oil during frying. A moderate heat of 150°C/300°F should be used for dense, uncooked food such as chicken joints, large fish or raw vegetables like artichokes. This ensures that the food is cooked right through before turning too brown. A higher heat of 170°C/325°F should be used for food already cooked, or light food dipped in batter or egg and breadcrumbs. A high temperature of 180°C/350°F should be used for very small pieces of food or tiny fish. Olive oil begins to smoke at 220°C/425°F, so it should not be allowed to reach this heat.

3 Olive oil should be carefully filtered after each use, and according to experts it is safe to re-use at least 10 times before its nutritional properties are impaired. I prefer to use the oil only 3 times to get a better flavor.

4 To deep-fry, slide the food gently into the hot oil, a few pieces at a time, to avoid cooling it down.

5 If the oil needs to be replenished, add the new oil when a batch of food is finished, and wait for it to reach the correct temperature before continuing with the frying.

6 When the food is ready, lift out with a slotted spoon (spatula), place on a paper towel to drain off any surplus oil, and serve at once.

RECIPES FOR STOCKS

In the past stocks were usually rich and elaborate, and cooks tended to use the same stock for every recipe, giving each dish a generic flavor. Today's tastes require lighter, healthier stocks, and I usually make a neutral light stock in large quantities and freeze it in 500ml/18 fl oz (2 cups) containers. I add appropriate herbs or flavors when reheating so that every dish has an individual, fresh taste.

Some commercially produced stocks are quite acceptable but be careful not to use them too often or all your rice dishes will have the same background taste.

Light Meat Stock

500g/1 lb 2 oz veal with bone or ½ chicken
1 onion, 2 carrots, 1 stick celery, roughly chopped
salt and 5 black peppercorns
1 litre/1¾ pints (4 cups) cold water

Put all the ingredients in a large saucepan and bring to a boil, skimming off any foam that rises to the surface. Cover and simmer for 2 hours. Herbs or other flavors can be added for the last 30 minutes. Allow to cool then skim any fat off the surface and strain.

Vegetable Stock

1 onion, 2 carrots, 1 stick celery, roughly chopped
1 leek, sliced
salt and 5 black peppercorns
1 clove garlic, crushed with the back of a knife
1 litre/1¾ pints (4 cups) cold water

Put all the ingredients in a large saucepan and bring to a boil. Cover and simmer for 2 hours. Herbs or other flavors can be added for the last 30 minutes. Allow to cool and strain.

Fish Stock

500g/1 lb 2 oz fish carcass, heads or available fish
1 onion, 1 carrot, 1 stick celery, roughly chopped
1 bay leaf
½ lemon
200ml/7 fl oz (1 cup) dry white wine if available
salt and black pepper

Put all the ingredients in a large saucepan and bring to a boil. Cover and simmer for 40 minutes. Herbs or other flavors can be added for the last 30 minutes. Allow to cool and strain.

Rich Meat Stock

500g/1 lb 2 oz red meat
250g/9 oz veal or chicken on the bone
1 onion, 2 carrots, 1 stick celery, roughly chopped
salt and 5 black peppercorns
1 litre/1¾ pints (4 cups) cold water

Method as for *Light Meat Stock* (page 5).

Note:
Green motif

〜〜〜

indicates vegetarian dishes

VEGETABLES

VEGETABLES

The sunny climate and mineral-rich volcanic soil give an intense flavor to Italian vegetables. The market stalls are a feast for the eye with their tender, mauve artichokes, opulent purple eggplants and lush, gaudy peppers. In autumn, orange pumpkins, tawny chestnuts and spectacular wild mushrooms dominate the scene, while in spring every shade of green is represented with asparagus, peas and fava beans.

The Italian way of eating places great emphasis on fresh vegetables and, as a result, frozen produce has made little headway, even in large towns. In today's more affluent climate, people eat more vegetables than meat through choice, not economic necessity, and the *cucina povera* tradition is still honored. Vegetables that accompany the main meal are always served on a separate plate and many of the best pasta and rice dishes are perfect for vegetarians.

RISOTTO CON ASPARAGI

≈

Asparagus Risotto

This delicate, creamy green risotto is one of my
favorites and during the asparagus season it can
be enjoyed all over Italy. It is a great
favorite in Venice.

SERVES 4

1kg/2 lb 4 oz green asparagus
pinch of salt
80g/3 oz (¾ stick) butter
1 medium onion, finely chopped
350g/12 oz (2 cups) Vialone nano rice (or Carnaroli or Arborio)
½ glass dry white wine
black pepper
50g/2 oz (generous ½ cup) freshly grated Parmesan

Break off the extreme tips (2 to 3cm/¾ to 1¼ in) of the asparagus and
keep to one side. Break off the tough inedible ends and discard. Break the
remaining stalk into 1 1/2 inch lengths and cook quickly in a little lightly
salted water. When they are tender, purée to make an asparagus stock and
bring to a boil.

Melt half the butter in a large pan and soften the onion in it before
adding the asparagus tips. With a wooden spoon stir in the rice and let it
absorb the flavor of the butter and onions before adding the wine. Turn
up the heat so that the wine evaporates quickly, then ladle on a
little of the boiling asparagus stock. When the rice has absorbed the
liquid stir in another ladle of stock and continue in this way until the
rice is cooked. You may need to use a little boiling water if the asparagus
stock is finished before the rice is tender. It is most important to add only
boiling stock, stirring in a little at a time to the rice. This process usually
takes about 20 minutes and needs constant care.

When the rice is cooked check for seasoning and stir in the remaining
butter and Parmesan. I usually add some freshly ground black pepper.

Minestra di Risi e Sparasi

Asparagus Broth

For this recipe you need thin, tender asparagus. In northern Italy the city of Bassano is famous for this type of asparagus and since we are in the Veneto, cream is an important ingredient!

Serves 4

500g/1 lb 2 oz thin green asparagus
50g/2 oz (½ stick) butter
1 onion, finely sliced
1.5 litres/2¾ pints (6 cups) light meat or vegetable stock
salt and black pepper
200g/7 oz (scant 1¼ cups) Vialone nano rice (or Carnaroli or Arborio)
50g/2 oz (generous ½ cup) freshly grated Parmesan
50ml/2 fl oz (scant ¼ cup) fresh double (heavy) cream
nutmeg for grating

Break off and discard the tough inedible part of the asparagus stalks. If the asparagus is very tender this might not be necessary. Break into lengths of about 1 inch. Heat half the butter in a large pan and gently cook the onion until soft. Add the asparagus, some of the stock and seasoning. Bring to a boil, cover and simmer for 10 minutes. Now pour in the rest of the stock, bring to a boil, add the rice and simmer for 15 to 20 minutes. When the rice is cooked, stir in 1 tablespoon of the Parmesan, the cream, the remaining butter and grate on a little nutmeg. Hand the rest of the cheese round at table.

Risotto con Carciofi

Artichoke Risotto

For this recipe use only tender young globe artichokes or small
frozen, trimmed ones. At Fini's restaurant in Modena, this
risotto is served garnished with crisp segments of fried
artichokes which make an interesting contrast
to the smooth, creamy risotto.

Serves 4

6 small tender globe artichokes
(Italian if possible), trimmed and sliced
juice of 1 lemon
1 litre/1¾ pints (4 cups) light meat or vegetable stock
50g/2 oz (½ stick) butter
1 small onion, finely chopped
salt and black pepper
350g/12 oz (2 cups) Carnaroli rice (or Vialone nano or Arborio)
1 tablespoon chopped fresh mint
50g/2 oz (generous ½ cup) freshly grated Parmesan

To trim artichokes, remove the tough outer leaves and cut off the spiky
tops. Cut the artichokes into quarters and remove the choke. Cut these
into thin vertical slices and put immediately into cold water and lemon
juice to prevent them from turning brown.

Heat the stock. Melt the butter in a large pan and gently fry the onion.
After a few minutes stir in the artichokes, season and pour in a little of
the boiling stock. Cover and cook gently for 10 minutes by which time the
liquid will have evaporated.

Now stir in the rice, using a wooden spoon, and start to add a little
more stock, a ladle at a time, waiting for the rice to absorb the liquid
before stirring in more. This process usually takes 20 minutes. When the
rice is barely cooked, sprinkle in the mint and correct the seasoning. Turn
off the heat, stir in the Parmesan and serve at once.

TIELLA DI RISO E CARCIOFI

≈≈

Artichoke and Rice Bake

Ostuni is a small medieval hilltop town in southern Puglia.
A sprawling new zone with comfortable modern hotels has grown
up by the sea, but Ostuni itself has remained intact with its labyrinthine
narrow streets and endless stone steps. In the past, the small houses were
whitewashed every year to help prevent the spread of pestilence, and seen
from the motorway, the town seems to float like a mirage above the
slopes of olive trees. The small *trattorie* serve interesting vegetable
dishes such as this one, unknown in the rest of Italy.

SERVES 4

6 small tender globe artichokes (Italian if possible), trimmed and sliced
salt and pepper
2 tablespoons freshly grated pecorino
200g/7 oz (scant 1¼ cups) Carnaroli rice (or Arborio or Vialone nano),
put to soak while preparing other ingredients
4 slices scamorza cheese
2 slices mozzarella
1 tablespoon finely chopped fresh parsley
2 cloves garlic, minced
½ dried chile pepper, minced
2 tablespoons extra virgin olive oil

Preheat the oven to 180°C/350°F and prepare the artichokes (see page
11). Remove half of them, rinse and pat dry. Arrange in a single layer in
the bottom of a lightly oiled ovenproof dish, preferably terra-cotta and
lightly season. Drain the rice and put the rice water to one side. Sprinkle
over half the pecorino and then the wet rice in a single layer. Lightly season and cover with the slices of cheese. Mix together the
parsley, garlic and chile and scatter over the cheese. Rinse and dry the
remaining artichokes and arrange over the top. Season and sprinkle over
the remaining pecorino. Drizzle over the oil and gently pour enough of
the rice water down the sides of the dish to come just below the cheese
topping to cook the rice.

Bake in the preheated oven for 45 minutes. Every 15 minutes check
the dish and, if necessary, add a little more hot water down the sides to
cook the rice. The finished dish should be firm with a golden crust.

Risotto con Zucchini e Melanzane

Zucchini and Eggplant Risotto

Zucchini and eggplant appear in
endless combinations in Mediterranean cooking. This is a southern
flavor used with rice in a northern Italy mode. Extra virgin olive oil
can be used instead of butter for the initial frying if preferred.

Serves 4

1 eggplant, sliced in 4 lengthwise and diced
coarse salt for purging
80g/3 oz (¾ stick) butter
1 celery stick, 1 carrot and 1 onion, finely sliced
1 tablespoon finely chopped fresh parsley
2 zucchinis, sliced in 4 lengthwise and diced
salt and black pepper
100ml/3½ fl oz (½ cup) dry white wine
2 ripe tomatoes, peeled, deseeded (see page 25) and chopped
4 fresh basil leaves, roughly torn
350g/12 oz (2 cups) Carnaroli rice (or Vialone nano or Arborio)
1.5 litres/2¾ pints (6 cups) stock
50g/2 oz (generous ½ cup) freshly grated Parmesan

Eggplants contain a bitter juice that can spoil the taste of a dish, so they
need to be purged before cooking. Arrange the sliced eggplant on a chop-
ping board. Sprinkle liberally with coarse salt and cover with another
board weighed down by a heavy pan. Fine salt should not be used as it is
too easily absorbed. After 30 minutes wash off the salt, rinse the eggplant
and pat dry with kitchen towel.

Heat half the butter in a large pan and gently cook the celery, carrot
and onion until soft. Stir in the parsley, zucchini and eggplant and
season. After cooking for 5 minutes, splash on the wine and add the
tomatoes and basil. Cook for a further 5 minutes and stir in the rice. Start
adding the boiling stock, a little at a time, waiting for the rice to absorb
the liquid before stirring in more. After 15 to 20 minutes, when the rice is
cooked *al dente* and the stock is absorbed, stir in the remaining butter and
Parmesan. Serve at once.

RISO E MELANZANE ALLA PALMERTINA

Baked Rice and Eggplant

Sicily has some delicious eggplant recipes. In Palermo, at the exciting *Vucciria* market which is always a blaze of color, I have seen a stall specializing in eggplants of every size and hue, just asking to be cooked. In fact, it is Palermo that gives us this rice version of *Melanzane alla Parmigiana*. The fresh tuma cheese does not seem to exist outside Sicily but it can be replaced with mozzarella.

SERVES 4

3 large eggplants, sliced
coarse salt for purging
plain (all-purpose) flour for dredging
oil for deep-frying
2 tablespoons extra virgin olive oil
1 small onion, finely chopped
350g/12 oz (2 cups) Arborio rice (or Carnaroli or Vialone nano)
1 litre/1¾ pints (4 cups) light meat or vegetable stock
50g/2 oz (½ stick) butter
1 tablespoon finely chopped fresh parsley
salt and black pepper
500ml/18 fl oz (2 cups) fresh tomato sauce (see page 15)
4 fresh basil leaves, roughly torn
100g/4 oz (1¼ cups) freshly grated caciocavallo cheese or Parmesan
200g/7 oz fresh tuma cheese or mozzarella, sliced

Preheat oven to 180°C/350°F and lightly oil a large ovenproof dish.

Purge the eggplants of their bitter juices (see page 13). Rinse, dry and lightly dredge in flour. Heat the olive oil in a deep-fryer, fry the eggplants slices in batches and leave to drain on kitchen paper.

Heat the olive oil in a large pan and gently fry the onion until soft. Stir in the rice and after 5 minutes pour in half the stock. Cook gently, adding more stock if necessary. After 10 minutes remove the rice from the heat. It should have absorbed the stock but still be very *al dente*. Stir in the butter and parsley. Season to taste.

Arrange a few slices of eggplant over the bottom of the ovenproof dish. Cover with one third of the tomato sauce, some basil, a little grated cheese and half the rice. Cover the rice with one third of the slices of cheese, half the remaining eggplant slices, half the remaining tomato sauce and some more grated cheese. Repeat the layers once more, finishing with the remaining cheese slices topped with the rest of the grated cheese. Bake for 15 minutes or until the top is golden brown.

Tomato Sauce

Many recipes call for a very small quantity of fresh tomato sauce. Tomato purée (paste) cannot be substituted. I suggest you make the full quantity of sauce and freeze it in small containers, to be defrosted and used as needed. It is better to use canned Italian plum tomatoes if you do not have ripe tomatoes full of flavor.

2 tablespoons extra virgin olive oil
1 small onion, finely chopped
2 x 400g/14 oz canned Italian plum tomates
4 fresh basil leaves, roughly torn
salt

Heat the oil in a shallow pan and gently cook the onion until soft. Add the tomatoes, basil and salt, and cook quickly until most of the juice has evaporated. Put through a food mill or mouli.

RISOTTO DI MELANZANE

Eggplant Risotto

In Italy we get eggplants of every hue, from white to deep purple. This risotto looks best with the smaller, violet colored variety. However it will taste good whatever the color if the eggplants are fresh. It is not worth making with dull, soft ones. Be sure to purge them in salt first to prevent their bitter juices from spoiling the risotto.

SERVES 4

300g/10½ oz small, firm, shiny eggplants, diced
coarse salt for purging
75g/3 oz (¾ stick) butter
2 tablespoons extra virgin olive oil
1 onion, finely chopped
1 clove garlic, finely chopped
300ml/10 fl oz (1¼ cups) fresh tomato sauce (see page 15)
350g/12 oz (2 cups) Carnaroli rice (or Vialone nano or Arborio)
1 litre/1¾ pints (4 cups) light meat or vegetable stock
1 tablespoon finely chopped fresh parsley
50g/2 oz (generous ½ cup) freshly grated Parmesan
black pepper

Purge the diced eggplants of their bitter juices (see page 13). Rinse well and pat dry.

Heat half the butter with the oil in a large pan and cook the onion, garlic and eggplants for 5 minutes. Stir in the tomato sauce followed by the rice and simmer for 5 minutes. Then add the stock gradually, a ladle at a time, as the liquid is absorbed by the rice. After about 20 minutes, when the rice is cooked and the stock absorbed, stir in the parsley, Parmesan and a little black pepper.

RISOTTO PREBOGGION

≈

Green Herb Risotto

In Liguria this risotto is made with *preboggion*, a bundle of mixed wild herbs which vary according to the season. Local lore has it that during the Crusades a Genovese lord, Goffredo di Buglione, sent his men out to scour the alien hills for fragrant herbs for his dinner. These herbs became known as *pro Buglione* which was corrupted to *preboggion*. For those of us who have to manage without a helpful army, I have suggested a good combination of herbs.

SERVES 4

2 tablespoons olive oil
1 clove garlic, minced
1 small onion, finely chopped
350g/12 oz (2 cups) Carnaroli rice (or Vialone nano or Arborio)
2 small zucchinis, diced
100g/4 oz cooked spinach, finely chopped
50g/2 oz finely chopped mixed fresh mint, sage and rosemary
30g/1 oz each finely chopped fresh basil, parsley and arugula
1 litre/1¾ pints (4 cups) light meat or vegetable stock
salt and black pepper
50g/2 oz (generous ½ cup) freshly grated Parmesan
30g/1 oz (¼ stick) butter

Heat the oil in a large pan and add the garlic and onion. When they are soft, add the rice and cook, stirring for 5 minutes so that it absorbs the oil. Now add the rest of the vegetables and herbs and gradually add the boiling stock, a ladle at a time, waiting for the rice to absorb the liquid before stirring in more. After about 20 minutes, when the rice is cooked, adjust the seasoning, stir in the cheese and butter, and serve at once.

Riso e Piselli col Pesto

Rice and Peas with Pesto

Although in Liguria they tell you pesto must be pounded by hand, today very few people have the time, arm muscles or inclination. In spring and summer when basil is in season, I make pesto several times a week, using my food processor to make a delicious sauce in less time than it takes to cook the pasta. I like to leave in some rough crumbs of Parmesan and pine nuts to give the sauce some texture. This recipe for home-made pesto can be found opposite.

Pesto was carried by the Genoese soldiers who took part in the Crusades and the same pungent sauce sustained the sailors on the great voyages of discovery that set sail from Liguria. Here, pesto adds another dimension to rice and peas.

Serves 4

50g/2 oz (½ stick) butter
50g/2 oz prosciutto, or bacon diced
1 medium onion, finely chopped
salt and black pepper
350g/12 oz (2 cups) Carnaroli rice (or Vialone nano or Arborio)
600g/1 lb 5 oz peas in pod or 250g/9 oz shelled
2 tablespoons spinach, chopped
2 tablespoons fresh pesto sauce (see opposite)
25g/1 oz (⅓ cup) freshly grated Parmesan

Melt the butter in a pan and gently cook the prosciutto or bacon with the onion. In a large saucepan bring about 750ml/1¼ pints (3 cups) water to a boil, add a pinch of salt and the rice and simmer for 10 minutes. Stir the peas and spinach into the rice and cook for another 7 minutes. Check the rice, which should be cooked but still *al dente*. Stir in the prosciutto mixture, pesto and cheese. Serve at once.

Pesto Sauce

2 cloves garlic
2 tablespoons pine nuts
4 tablespoons roughly chopped Parmesan
1 large bunch fresh basil
salt and black pepper
75ml/2½ fl oz (⅓ cup) extra virgin olive oil

Chop the garlic, pine nuts and Parmesan in a food processor. Wash the basil leaves and pat them dry. Add them to the food processor with the seasoning, switch on and slowly pour in the oil to make a sauce which still has some texture from the Parmesan and pine nuts.

MINESTRA DI RISO E ZUCCHINI

Rice and Zucchini Broth

It is only worth doing this *minestra* if you have young, firm zucchinis. Once they have become soft they tend to taste bitter.

SERVES 4

50g/2 oz (½ stick) butter
1 onion, finely chopped
250g/9 oz zucchini, diced or thinly sliced
1.2 litres/2 pints (5 cups) light meat or vegetable stock
200g/7 oz (scant 1¼ cups) Carnaroli rice (or Vialone nano or Arborio)
50g/2 oz (generous ½ cup) freshly grated Parmesan
salt and black pepper
1 tablespoon chopped fresh parsley

Heat the butter in a large pan and cook the onion until soft. Add the zucchinis and stir around the pan for 5 minutes. Pour over the boiling stock and stir in the rice. Bring to a boil and simmer for 15 to 20 minutes. Check the seasoning and stir in the Parmesan and parsley. Serve immediately.

RISO E FASOI ALLA FRIULANA

Rice and Bean Broth

In Friuli the winters are cold and this warming *minestra* helps to keep the chill out of the bones, especially if served with a glass of robust Friuli red wine.

SERVES 4

1 tablespoon extra virgin olive oil
100g/4 oz bacon, chopped
1 onion, finely chopped
1 celery stick, finely chopped
150g/5½ oz dried beans, soaked overnight
200g/7 oz potatoes, peeled and cubed
1 bay leaf
1.5 litres/2¾ pints (6 cups) stock
200g/7 oz (scant 1¼ cups) Vialone nano rice (or Cararoli or Arborio)
black pepper
50g/2 oz (generous ½ cup) freshly grated Parmesan (optional)

Heat the oil in a large pan and gently cook the bacon, onion and celery until soft. Add the drained beans, potatoes and the bay leaf. Pour over the boiling stock and gently simmer for 2 hours. When the beans start to disintegrate at the edges pour in the rice. Simmer for 15 to 20 minutes more, then season with black pepper. The cheese can be handed round at table if desired.

Minestra di Riso e Cime di Rape

Broccoli and Rice Broth

In Puglia turnips are grown for their tops, and these pungent greens are used in many dishes. This *minestra* comes from northern Puglia, near Foggia.

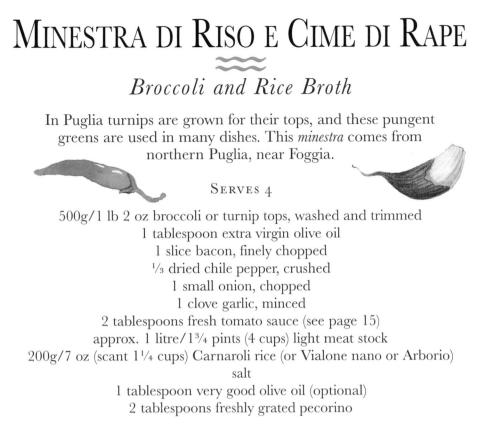

Serves 4

500g/1 lb 2 oz broccoli or turnip tops, washed and trimmed
1 tablespoon extra virgin olive oil
1 slice bacon, finely chopped
1/3 dried chile pepper, crushed
1 small onion, chopped
1 clove garlic, minced
2 tablespoons fresh tomato sauce (see page 15)
approx. 1 litre/1¾ pints (4 cups) light meat stock
200g/7 oz (scant 1¼ cups) Carnaroli rice (or Vialone nano or Arborio)
salt
1 tablespoon very good olive oil (optional)
2 tablespoons freshly grated pecorino

If using broccoli, divide into florets. Heat the oil in a large pan and gently stew the bacon, chile, onion and garlic. Let the onion and garlic soften without changing color. Stir in the tomato sauce and the broccoli or turnip tops. After a few minutes add about 250ml/9 fl oz (generous 1 cup) boiling stock and the rice. Stir from time to time and add more stock as needed. Simmer for about 25 minutes. The *minestra* should be thick but liquid. Add salt if needed but remember the pecorino is salty. Drizzle on a little good olive oil if you wish, and sprinkle on the cheese. If you use the oil you will need less cheese.

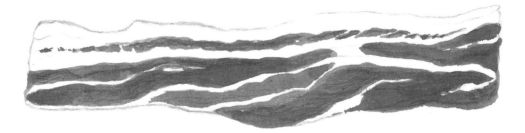

Minestra Napoletana

Neapolitan Rice and Savoy Cabbage Broth

This is a really comforting *minestra* to have on a chilly evening, and it heats up well for next day's quick lunch.

Serves 4

1 tablespoon extra virgin olive oil
100g/4 oz bacon, diced
1 small onion, finely chopped
1 clove garlic, minced
⅓ dried chile pepper
1.2 litres/2 pints (5 cups) light meat stock or water
1 small savoy cabbage, stalk and ribs removed, cut into strips
200g/7 oz (scant 1¼ cups) Carnaroli rice (or Vialone nano or Arborio)
100g/4 oz caciocavallo or provolone cheese, diced
2 tablespoons freshly grated Parmesan
1 tablespoon freshly grated pecorino
salt

Heat the oil in a large pan and gently cook the bacon, onion and garlic until soft. Crumple in the chile pepper. Heat half the stock or salted water and when it begins to boil stir in the cabbage and the onion mixture. Pour in the rice and stir well. Simmer for about 25 minutes, adding more stock or water as necessary. The broth should be thick but liquid.

A few minutes before removing the *minestra* from the heat, stir in the diced cheese. Remove from the heat, stir in the grated cheese, adjust salt and serve.

RISI COI FENOCI

≈

Fennel Risotto

In Venice this risotto is enjoyed for its delicate flavor, and often served as a panacea for the digestion disturbed by over-indulgence. But beware! The intriguing taste provokes the appetite and, the first time I sampled it, I kept coming back for another spoonful.

SERVES 4

80g/3 oz (¾ stick) butter
1 small onion, finely sliced
1 large fennel bulb with leaves, cut into thin strips
350g/12 oz (2 cups) Vialone nano rice (or Carnaroli or Arborio)
1 litre/1¾ pints (4 cups) light meat or vegetable stock
4 teaspoons freshly grated Parmesan
salt and black pepper

Heat half the butter in a large pan and gently cook the onion and fennel for 15 minutes. Do not let them change color. Add the rice and cook for about 5 minutes in the fennel and onion mixture, stirring continuously. Boil the stock and gradually add it to the pan, a ladle at a time, waiting for the rice to absorb the stock before stirring in more. After about 20 minutes the rice will be cooked but quite liquid – *all'onda* (see page 4). Beat in the remaining butter and all the Parmesan, season with salt, add the freshly ground black pepper and serve at once.

MINESTRA DI PORRI E RISO

Leek and Rice Broth

Today, Asti, in Piemonte, is renowned for its good food and associated with great gastronomic delights, but at one time the local produce was almost exclusively garlic and leeks. This recipe was a firm local favorite in the Middle Ages, when it was believed that leeks cleansed the blood. Whatever its medicinal properties, this is a tasty, economical broth that brings instant comfort when the chill in the air suggests the misty autumn days that gave the Piemontese wine, Nebbiolo, its name.

SERVES 4

100g/4 oz (1 stick) butter
300g/10½ oz leeks, cleaned and sliced into rings
1 thin slice bacon, chopped (optional)
1 clove garlic, finely chopped
1 bay leaf
150g/5½ oz potatoes, peeled and chopped
1.5 litres/2¾ pints (6 cups) boiling water
salt and black pepper
300g/10½ oz (1⅔ cups) Carnaroli rice (or Vialone nano or Arborio)
nutmeg for grating
75g/3 oz Gruyère, diced
75g/3 oz fontina cheese, diced

Melt half the butter in a large pan and add half the leeks together with the chopped bacon, garlic and bay leaf. Cover and stew over a low heat for 20 minutes. Now add the remaining leeks, the potato and the boiling water. Simmer for 15 minutes, season to taste and stir in the rice. Grate in a little nutmeg. When the rice is cooked, mash the potatoes with a wooden spoon and stir in the diced cheeses and the remaining butter. Check the seasoning before serving.

Minestra di Riso e Lenticchie

Rice and Lentil Broth

Umbria does not use rice a great deal but this *minestra* is Umbrian and is best made with the Castelnuovo lentils from Norcia.

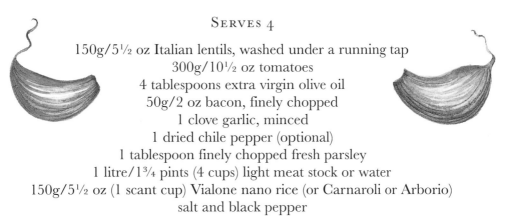

Serves 4

150g/5½ oz Italian lentils, washed under a running tap
300g/10½ oz tomatoes
4 tablespoons extra virgin olive oil
50g/2 oz bacon, finely chopped
1 clove garlic, minced
1 dried chile pepper (optional)
1 tablespoon finely chopped fresh parsley
1 litre/1¾ pints (4 cups) light meat stock or water
150g/5½ oz (1 scant cup) Vialone nano rice (or Carnaroli or Arborio)
salt and black pepper

Cook the lentils in unsalted water until soft, drain and set aside. The time will depend on the age of the lentils. If they are fresh it should take 20 minutes. Blanch the tomatoes quickly in boiling water. The skins can then be easily removed. To deseed, cut the tomatoes into quarters and scoop out the seeds with a small knife.

Heat the olive oil in a large pan and gently cook the bacon and garlic until the fat runs out of the bacon. Crumble the dried chile in if you would like a touch of spice. Stir in the tomatoes and parsley and cook for 5 minutes before adding the stock or water. Bring to a boil, pour in the rice and after 10 minutes add the lentils. Simmer for another 10 minutes, check the seasoning and serve.

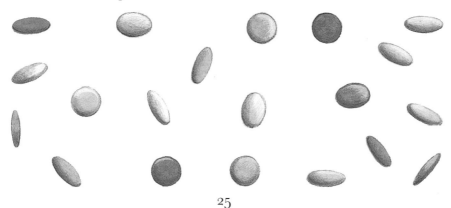

Risotto con i Funghi

Wild Mushroom Risotto

This risotto really needs some tasty wild mushrooms mixed with field mushrooms to give it an authentic flavor. Wild mushrooms should be sponged but not immersed in water. Dried porcini mushrooms should be soaked for 15 minutes in tepid water, then the water should be poured through a strainer to remove grit, and added to the stock.

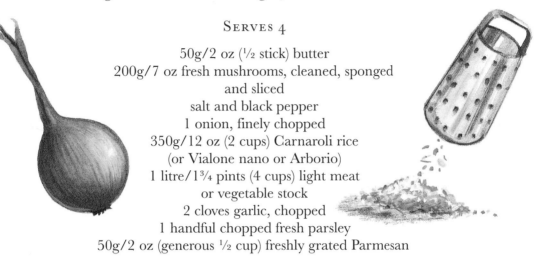

Serves 4

50g/2 oz (½ stick) butter
200g/7 oz fresh mushrooms, cleaned, sponged
and sliced
salt and black pepper
1 onion, finely chopped
350g/12 oz (2 cups) Carnaroli rice
(or Vialone nano or Arborio)
1 litre/1¾ pints (4 cups) light meat
or vegetable stock
2 cloves garlic, chopped
1 handful chopped fresh parsley
50g/2 oz (generous ½ cup) freshly grated Parmesan

Melt half the butter in a pan and gently cook the mushrooms with a little salt and pepper. In your risotto pan melt the remaining butter and gently cook the onion until soft. Stir in the rice and let it absorb some of the flavor before adding the boiling stock, a ladle at a time, waiting for the rice to absorb the liquid before stirring in more. After about 15 minutes check the seasoning and stir in the mushrooms, garlic and parsley. When the rice is still *all'onda* (see page 4) remove from the heat and stir in the Parmesan.

RISOTTO ALLA CIPOLLA

Onion Risotto

I arrived in Mantova by very slow train from Parma one cold January evening in a dense fog, reminiscent of the London pea-soupers of my childhood. Abandoning my original plan to take a taxi to a famous restaurant in an outlying village, desperate for warmth and comfort, I went towards the welcoming light of a humble *trattoria*. I was served this onion risotto and I savored each spoonful with a contented smile on my face. The risotto must be served *all'onda* (see page 4).

SERVES 4

50g/2 oz (½ stick) butter
3 white onions, finely chopped
150ml/5 fl oz (⅔ cup) dry white wine
salt and black pepper
350g/12 oz (2 cups) Vialone nano rice (or Carnaroli or Arborio)
1 litre/1¾ pints (4 cups) light meat or vegetable stock
150ml/5 fl oz (⅔ cup) double (heavy) cream
50g/2 oz (generous ½ cup) freshly grated Parmesan

Heat half the butter in a pan and gently cook the onions until soft. Pour in half the wine and use a blender or food processor to make a smooth sauce. Season to taste. Heat the remaining butter in a large pan and stir the rice around it for 5 minutes. Pour in the rest of the wine and continue stirring until it has almost evaporated. Then stir in the boiling stock and onion sauce a little at a time, waiting for the liquid to be absorbed before stirring in more. When the rice is cooked, after about 15 to 20 minutes, stir in the cream, Parmesan and some black pepper and serve.

RISI E BISI

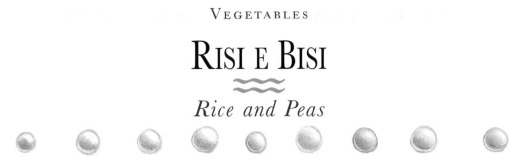

Rice and Peas

This Venetian dish used to be served to the *doge* on 25 April,
St Mark's Day. It was immortalized by Rossini in the *Risi* chorus in
his opera *Tancredi*. He composed the chorus while patiently waiting for his
Risi e Bisi to be cooked in his favorite Venetian *trattoria*.
The dish is traditionally made with the first sweet young peas of
the season. However it can be made very successfully with frozen peas
instead if a well-flavored stock is used. If you do have fresh young peas,
cook some of the washed, empty pods in lightly salted, boiling water
to make the stock. *Risi e Bisi* is meant to be more liquid, resembling
a dense broth rather than a risotto.

SERVES 4

80g/3 oz (¾ stick) butter
1 small onion, finely chopped
50g/2 oz prosciutto, ham or bacon, finely chopped
1kg/2 lb 4 oz fresh young unshelled peas or 400g/14 oz shelled or frozen peas
1 litre/1¾ pints (4 cups) light meat stock
300g/10½ oz (1⅔ cups) Vialone nano rice (or Carnaroli or Arborio)
50g/2 oz (generous ½ cup) freshly grated Parmesan
salt and black pepper

Melt half the butter in a large pan and stir in the finely chopped onion and
prosciutto, ham or bacon. After a few minutes add the shelled or frozen
peas and two ladles of boiling water. If the peas are not young and sweet
add a pinch of sugar. Cover and cook for 5 minutes or a little longer if the
peas are rather large. Add the stock and bring to a boil. Pour in the rice
and simmer, stirring occasionally to check that you do not need more
liquid. When the rice is cooked stir in the remaining butter and the freshly
grated cheese. Check the seasoning and grind a little black pepper on top.

Risotto alle Primizie

Risotto with Spring Vegetables

'Aimo e Nadia' is my favorite restaurant in Milan, and I always find I am smiling as I enjoy Aimo and Nadia's cooking. They use superb ingredients in a creative way that is never exaggerated for the sake of striking an innovative note. They achieve this effect with a masterly simplicity that should inspire anyone hoping to produce good Italian food.

Serves 4

100g/4 oz shelled fava beans
100g/4 oz shelled peas
30g/1 oz young carrots, cut into small batons
30g/1 oz small zucchinis, cut into batons
350g/12 oz (2 cups) Carnaroli rice (or Vialone nano or Arborio)
4 tablespoons extra virgin olive oil
salt and black pepper
300g/10½ oz ripe tomatoes
200g/7 oz fresh ricotta cheese, at room temperature
8 basil leaves

Cook the spring vegetables for 10 minutes in a pan of lightly salted boiling water, drain and keep warm. Chop the tomatoes and sieve or pass through a food mill.

Bring 700ml/1¼ pints (3 cups) lightly salted water to a boil in another pan and cook the rice for 15 to 20 minutes. When the water has all been absorbed, stir in half the oil and the seasoning and arrange the rice on individual plates.

Spoon some of the puréed tomato on the center of each portion and arrange the ricotta on top. Shred the basil and sprinkle over the top of each portion. Dress the drained spring vegetables with the remaining olive oil and scatter over the rice.

Peperoni al Riso

≋

Peppers Stuffed with Rice

These (bell or sweet) peppers make a colorful contribution
to the *antipasto* table.

Serves 4

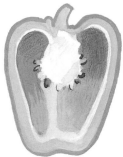

200g/7 oz (scant 1¼ cups) Carnaroli rice
(or Vialone nano or Arborio)
50g/2 oz (½ stick) butter
2 teaspoons finely chopped fresh parsley
salt and black pepper
4 large red or yellow (bell or sweet) peppers
2 tablespoons fresh dried breadcrumbs
2 tablespoons extra virgin olive oil
2 cloves garlic, finely chopped
4 anchovy fillets, chopped
30g/1 oz (⅓ cup) freshly grated pecorino (optional)

Preheat oven to 175°C/350°F and grease a large ovenproof dish.

Bring 500ml/18 fl oz (2 cups) lightly salted water to a boil and
cook the rice for 10 minutes. Drain and stir in the butter, parsley and
seasoning.

Cut the peppers in half horizontally and remove the seeds and tough
fibers. Arrange them in the ovenproof dish and spoon the rice into each
half. Sprinkle over the breadcrumbs.

Heat the oil in a pan and gently cook the garlic and anchovy,
pressing the fillets with the back of a wooden spoon. When the anchovy
has 'melted' into the oil, remove from the heat and pour over the peppers.
If using pecorino it can be sprinkled on top before baking for 25 minutes.

Risi e Peperoni

Rice with Sweet Peppers

Another attractive tasty dish from the Veneto region, *Risi e Peperoni* has become a great family favorite and I have successfully introduced it to many Romans. I suspect they increase the amount of olive oil since butter is not used for cooking further south.

Serves 4

1 firm red (bell or sweet) pepper
1 firm yellow (bell or sweet) pepper
50g/2 oz (½ stick) butter
2 tablespoons extra virgin olive oil
1 onion, finely sliced
1 tablespoon finely chopped fresh parsley
4 basil leaves, torn into pieces
1 clove garlic, minced
salt and black pepper
350g/12 oz (2 cups) Vialone nano rice (or Carnaroli or Arborio)
30g/1 oz (⅓ cup) freshly grated Parmesan (optional)

Roast the peppers over a high flame or grill to blister the skins. Remove skins, seeds and tough internal fibers. Cut into strips. Heat half the butter and olive oil in a pan and gently fry the onion until it is soft. Stir in the herbs, garlic and peppers, season and cook gently. Boil the rice separately in a large pan in lightly salted water until cooked (see page 4). Drain and stir in the remaining butter and the pepper mixture. Check seasoning and serve at once. Parmesan can be served separately if desired.

TIELLA DI PATATE, RISO E POMODORINI

Potato, Rice and Tomato Bake

This versatile recipe can be served as a one-dish vegetarian meal or a starter or vegetable side dish. It is usually eaten at room temperature when all the flavors have blended together, but it is equally good hot or cold. In Puglia, it is a tradition to drizzle over the oil in a sign of the cross.

SERVES 4

2 tablespoons finely grated pecorino
2 cloves garlic, minced
1 tablespoon chopped fresh parsley
500g/1 lb 2 oz potatoes, thinly sliced
salt and black pepper
1 large onion, thinly sliced
200g/7 oz cherry tomatoes, halved
200g/7 oz (scant 1¼ cups) Arborio rice (or Carnaroli or Vialone nano),
put to soak while preparing other ingredients
2 tablespoons extra virgin olive oil

Preheat the oven to 170°C/325°F and lightly oil a large ovenproof dish, preferably terra-cotta.

Mix together the pecorino, garlic and parsley, or blend in a food processor. Make an overlapping layer of half the potato slices in the oven dish. Season with salt and pepper. Cover with a similar layer of half the onion and arrange half the tomatoes over the top. Drain the rice but keep the water. Scatter half the rice over the tomato layer and sprinkle with half the pecorino mixture. Drizzle over half the olive oil.

Reserve the remaining tomatoes but repeat the other layers, finishing with the pecorino mixture. Arrange the tomatoes over the top and gently pour the rice water down the sides of the dish so that it comes to just below the cheese topping. The rice and potatoes need water to cook.

Drizzle over the remaining olive oil and bake for about 40 minutes. After 20 minutes check to see if the dish looks dry and, if necessary, add a little hot water down the sides.

The final dish should be moist but crisp on top.

RISO E PATATE

Potato and Rosemary Risotto

In Italy potatoes are combined with rice or pizza in a number of delicious dishes, but non-Italians have to overcome their initial resistance to the idea. I am an ardent convert and I have a passion for the Pugliese *tielle* (see page 33), and the Roman pizza *rustica* topped with potato and rosemary. In Venice, *Riso e Patate* is enjoyed during the cold, damp months, and since I am a fan of Donna Leon's thrillers I can imagine the Brunetti family savoring this risotto for lunch during the *acqua alta* (floods).

SERVES 4

50g/2 oz (½ stick) butter
50g/2 oz bacon, diced
3 medium potatoes, peeled and cubed
1 onion, finely sliced
2 teaspoons chopped fresh rosemary
1 tablespoon finely chopped fresh parsley
300g/10½ oz (1⅔ cups) Vialone nano rice (or Carnaroli or Arborio)
1.5 litres/2¾ pints (6 cups) light meat stock
salt and black pepper
50g/2 oz (generous ½ cup) freshly grated Parmesan

Melt half the butter in a large pan and stir in the bacon and potato. After 5 minutes add the onion and herbs. Stir and cook gently for another 5 minutes. Stir in the rice and let it absorb the flavors for about 5 minutes. Add the boiling stock, ladle by ladle, waiting for the rice to absorb the liquid before stirring in more. When the risotto is cooked but still *al dente* and liquid, check the seasoning and stir in the remaining butter and half the Parmesan. Serve the remaining cheese at table.

Riso e Zucca

≈

Rice with Pumpkin

Many years ago, when I lived in England, the name 'Mantova' conjured up immediate thoughts of Romeo's banishment from Verona, but nowadays literary memories have been ousted by culinary reminiscences, for the city and surrounding small towns are home to some of Italy's finest restaurants. Pumpkin is found in many guises and this subtle dish reflects the high standards of the fifteenth-century, ruling Gonzaga family.

Serves 4

50g/2 oz (½ stick) butter
1 small onion, 1 carrot and 1 celery stick, finely chopped
1 slice bacon, finely chopped (optional)
400g/14 oz pumpkin, peeled, cleaned, sliced and roughly chopped
1 litre/1¾ pints (4 cups) light meat stock
350g/12 oz (2 cups) Vialone nano rice (or Carnaroli or Arborio)
salt and black pepper
50g/2 oz (generous ½ cup) freshly grated Parmesan

Heat half the butter and gently fry the onion, carrot and celery. Stir frequently and cook until the vegetables are soft enough to be sieved or passed through a food mill.

In a heavy bottomed saucepan, melt the remaining butter and gently stir fry the bacon and pumpkin. Do not let them change color. Boil the stock and pour on to the pumpkin with the sieved vegetable mixture, then add the rice. Cook for about 15 minutes, stirring frequently as the mixture becomes thicker. Add a little more stock or boiling water if necessary. The rice should not be too dense.

Adjust seasoning, turn off the heat and stir in half the Parmesan. Serve immediately with the remaining Parmesan passed round with the pepper mill.

RISOTTO AI POMODORI AL FORNO

≈

Roasted Tomato Risotto

For this dish you need to have full-flavored, ripe, red tomatoes.
The chef, Patrizio Cesarini, at the hotel 'Palazzo Terranova' in Umbria
made this risotto for me, using the tomatoes and basil from his
vegetable garden. I found it very exciting, and afterwards I wondered if
the magic of the Terranova terrace, and the moonlight, had woven a
special spell. As soon as I came back to Rome, I made it for some Italian
friends and they were enchanted, even without the Umbrian landscape.
In Italy pasta with tomatoes is an everyday dish but it is unusual to find
a tomato risotto, and roasted, they have a very special flavor.

SERVES 4

6 large red tomatoes, halved
salt and black pepper
6 basil leaves, torn in half
2 cloves garlic, each sliced into 6 pieces
2 tablespoons extra virgin olive oil
1 onion, finely chopped
350g/12 oz (2 cups) Carnaroli rice (or Vialone nano or Arborio)
1 litre/1¾ pints (4 cups) light meat or vegetable stock
Parmesan for grating

Preheat the oven to 240°C/475°F. Arrange the tomato halves in a single
layer in a roasting tin. Season and put a piece of basil and garlic on each
half and roast for 15 minutes. Remove from the oven and lift the tomatoes out of the tin with a slotted spoon. Discard the skins, basil and garlic, and chop the pulp.

    Heat the oil in a large pan and cook the onion until soft. Add the rice
and stir around the pan for 5 minutes. Stir in the boiling stock, a ladle at
a time, waiting for the rice to absorb the liquid before stirring in more.
After 15 minutes, when the rice is nearly cooked, stir in the tomatoes and
continue stirring for another 5 minutes until the rice is *al dente*. Serve with
the Parmesan to be freshly grated over the risotto at table.

RISOTTO CON GLI SPINACI

≈≈

Spinach Risotto

This risotto comes from Tuscany and I first sampled it at 'La Chiusa' restaurant in Montefollonico. The finished dish is an appealing green. Other leafy greens can be used instead of spinach.

SERVES 4

500g/1 lb 2 oz fresh spinach
100g/4 oz (1 stick) butter
50g/2 oz (generous ½ cup) freshly grated Parmesan
pinch of grated nutmeg
salt
1 onion, finely chopped
350g/12 oz (2 cups) Vialone nano rice (or Carnaroli or Arborio)
1 litre/1¾ pints (4 cups) light meat or vegetable stock

Wash the spinach and cook quickly in a covered pan in the water clinging to the leaves. Drain well then process or sieve to a fine purée. Heat half the butter in a pan, add 2 tablespoons of the Parmesan and stir in the spinach with a pinch of grated nutmeg and a little salt. Stir well and put to one side. Heat half the remaining butter in a large pan and gently cook the onion until soft. Add the rice and stir for 5 minutes, then start adding the stock a ladle at a time, waiting for the rice to absorb the liquid before stirring in more. When the rice is nearly cooked after about 15 minutes, stir in the spinach and cook for a few minutes more. Stir in the remaining butter and Parmesan and serve.

MINESTRA MARIA

Spinach and Egg Broth

I have not been able to find the Maria who gives her name to this *minestra* from Piemonte. It does not seem to be associated with the feast of the Assumption of the Virgin Mary, celebrated on August 15.

SERVES 4

500g/1 lb 2 oz spinach
50g/2 oz (½ stick) butter
salt and black pepper
1 litre/1¾ pints (4 cups) light meat or vegetable stock
200g/7 oz (scant 1¼ cups) Carnaroli rice (or Vialone nano or Arborio)
1 fresh egg
50g/2 oz (generous ½ cup) freshly grated Parmesan

Wash the spinach, shake dry and cut into ribbons. Melt the butter in a large pan and stir in the spinach. Continue stirring for 4 to 5 minutes until cooked. Season to taste.

Take 100ml/4 fl oz (½ cup) of the stock and put to one side. Bring the rest to a boil in another pan and add the spinach. Bring back to a boil, add the rice and simmer uncovered for 15 to 20 minutes until the rice is cooked.

Beat the egg with 1 tablespoon Parmesan and the reserved cold stock. Pour into a soup tureen and stir in the rice and spinach. The rest of the Parmesan can be passed round at table.

TORTA VERDE

Spinach and Rice Tart

This baked rice dish can be prepared in advance which makes it ideal for dinner parties. It looks very attractive, and spinach, rice and cheese are a winning combination. Any leafy vegetable can be used to make this Piemonte *torta*.

SERVES 4

30g/1 oz (¼ stick) butter
3 leeks, cleaned and cut into rings
2 cloves garlic, finely chopped
50g/2 oz bacon, chopped
1 kg/2 lb 4 oz spinach, trimmed, washed and roughly chopped
salt and black pepper
150g/5½ oz (1 scant cup) Carnaroli rice (or Vialone nano or Arborio)
600ml/1 pint (2½ cups) light meat stock
4 eggs, beaten
30g/1 oz (⅓ cup) freshly grated Parmesan
pinch of grated nutmeg
fresh breadcrumbs, toasted
30g/1 oz (¼ stick) butter for the topping

Preheat the oven to 200°C/400°F. In a large pan or wok melt the butter and stew the leeks until they are soft. Add the garlic and bacon and, as they begin to turn color, stir in the roughly chopped spinach and a little salt and pepper. Cook gently and when the spinach is reduced, stir in the rice and a ladle of boiling stock. Add a ladle of stock from time to time until the rice is cooked. All the liquid must be absorbed, but the rice must remain firm (*al dente*) so you need to be sparing with the stock.

Remove from the heat and stir in the eggs, cheese and some grated nutmeg. Butter a flat, round ovenproof dish and dust with breadcrumbs. Spoon in the spinach mixture, levelling off the top. Sprinkle with more breadcrumbs and dot with butter. Bake for 30 minutes.

Risotto Cinque Terre

Risotto from the Cinque Terre

The Cinque Terre are the five small fishing villages perched precariously on the cliffs near Portovenere in Liguria, where the Appenines come right down to the sea. They are opposite Lerici and the beautiful bay named Golfo dei Poeti after Shelley and Byron.

Serves 4

2 cloves garlic
1 handful of basil leaves
salt
350g/12 oz tomatoes, peeled (see page 25),
chopped and sieved
2 tablespoons extra virgin olive oil
30g/1 oz pine nuts
350g/12 oz (2 cups) Carnaroli rice (or Vialone nano or Arborio)
150ml/5 fl oz (²⁄₃ cup) dry white wine
1 litre/1¾ pints (4 cups) light meat or vegetable stock
40g/1½ oz (⅓ stick) butter
30g/1 oz (⅓ cup) freshly grated pecorino

Chop the garlic and basil with a little salt to keep the basil green. I usually use the small bowl of my food processor, but of course in Liguria they expect you to use a pestle and mortar. Gently heat the sieved tomatoes in a pan and stir in the basil mixture. Simmer for 10 minutes.

Heat the oil in another pan and stir in the pine nuts. When they begin to turn color add the rice and stir around the pan for 5 minutes before pouring in the wine. Continue stirring until the wine has almost evaporated before starting to add the stock a ladle at a time, waiting for the rice to absorb the liquid before stirring in more. After 10 minutes stir in the tomato mixture and go on adding stock until the risotto is cooked. Remove from the heat and stir in the butter and pecorino. Serve at once.

Pomodori al Riso

Baked Tomatoes Stuffed with Rice

This is a great Roman favorite. During the summer months the street markets have wooden crates full of perfect large, round, red tomatoes with the scrawled, laconic message *di riso*.

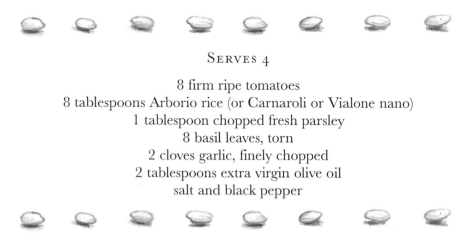

Serves 4

8 firm ripe tomatoes
8 tablespoons Arborio rice (or Carnaroli or Vialone nano)
1 tablespoon chopped fresh parsley
8 basil leaves, torn
2 cloves garlic, finely chopped
2 tablespoons extra virgin olive oil
salt and black pepper

Preheat the oven to 180°C/350°F and lightly oil an ovenproof dish just big enough to hold the 8 tomatoes.

Slice off the top of each tomato and keep to use as a lid. With a teaspoon scoop out the pulp without damaging the walls and blend in a food processor. Mix with the remaining ingredients except for the oil. Half fill the tomatoes with the mixture, replacing the tops as lids. Arrange in the dish and drizzle a little oil over the tops. Bake for about 50 minutes then remove from the oven and leave to stand before serving at room temperature from the baking dish.

Risotto con il Radicchio di Treviso

Risotto with Radicchio

Cooked radicchio tends to be a little bitter, but the Parmesan gives a more rounded taste. Bitter leaves are very pleasing to the Italian palate.

Serves 4

50g/2 oz (½ stick) butter
50g/2 oz prosciutto or bacon, diced
1 onion, finely chopped
1 clove garlic, minced
1 fresh sage leaf
2 teaspoons fresh chopped rosemary
250g/9 oz radicchio, trimmed and cut into strips
1 litre/1¾ pints (4 cups) light meat stock
350g/12 oz (2 cups) Vialone nano rice (or Carnaroli or Arborio)
salt and black pepper
50g/2 oz (generous ½ cup) freshly grated Parmesan

Heat half the butter in a pan and cook the prosciutto or bacon, onion, garlic and herbs for 10 minutes, stirring all the time. Add the radicchio and 2 tablespoons of the stock. Cook gently for another 10 minutes then stir in the rice. Gradually add the boiling stock a ladle at a time, waiting for the rice to absorb the liquid before stirring in more. Stir continually and when the rice is cooked, but *all'onda* (see page 4), check the seasoning and stir in the Parmesan.

INSALATA ALLA NAPOLETANA

≈≈≈

Neapolitan Rice Salad

This tomato dressing is used for both rice and pasta salads.
It is usually prepared in July and August when the tomatoes are ripe
and full of flavor. Do not attempt the recipe with winter tomatoes.
It is important to prepare the tomatoes and mix with the rice
3 or 4 hours in advance.

SERVES 4

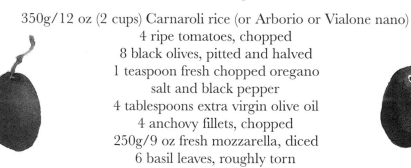

350g/12 oz (2 cups) Carnaroli rice (or Arborio or Vialone nano)
4 ripe tomatoes, chopped
8 black olives, pitted and halved
1 teaspoon fresh chopped oregano
salt and black pepper
4 tablespoons extra virgin olive oil
4 anchovy fillets, chopped
250g/9 oz fresh mozzarella, diced
6 basil leaves, roughly torn

Cook the rice in double its quantity of boiling salted water. After 15
minutes drain any remaining water and spread the rice out on a plate to
cool. Transfer to a salad bowl and stir in the tomatoes, olives, oregano,
seasoning and olive oil. Just before serving stir in the anchovies,
mozzarella and basil.

RISOTTO AL POMODORO

~~~

Tomato Risotto

If you prefer you can pass the tomatoes through a food mill, or sieve to remove the seeds. I usually just chop them because this is an 'every day' risotto, and the family don't seem to object to the seeds!

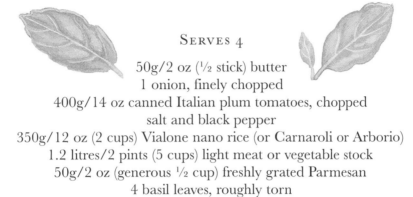

SERVES 4

50g/2 oz (½ stick) butter
1 onion, finely chopped
400g/14 oz canned Italian plum tomatoes, chopped
salt and black pepper
350g/12 oz (2 cups) Vialone nano rice (or Carnaroli or Arborio)
1.2 litres/2 pints (5 cups) light meat or vegetable stock
50g/2 oz (generous ½ cup) freshly grated Parmesan
4 basil leaves, roughly torn

Heat the butter in a large pan and gently cook the onion until soft. Stir in the tomatoes, season, and cook for about 10 to 15 minutes. Add the rice and cook, stirring, for 5 minutes. Then start adding the boiling stock a ladle at a time, waiting for the rice to absorb the liquid before stirring in more. After 15 to 20 minutes, when the rice is cooked but still *al dente* and the stock is absorbed, remove from the heat and stir in the Parmesan and basil. Serve at once.

RIS IN CAGNOUN

Rice with Brown Butter

In Lombardy, this dish has a rather off-putting name. The dark butter flecks the white rice grains, and years ago it obviously reminded someone of the little white worms with black eyes called *cagnott* in dialect. Those of us who don't understand the local foibles can enjoy this delicious rice without a hint of repugnance! I often serve it as a quick, simple accompaniment to a main meal.

SERVES 4

400g/14 oz (2⅓ cups) Carnaroli rice (or Vialone nano or Arborio)
125g/4½ oz (1⅛ sticks) butter
1 clove garlic, crushed with the back of a knife
4 sage leaves
50g/2 oz (generous ½ cup) freshly grated Parmesan
salt

Bring a large pan of lightly salted water to a boil. Pour in the rice and simmer for 10 minutes until it is *al dente* and drain.

While the rice is cooking, heat the butter in another pan and add the garlic and sage. Let the butter go brown but not burned. Discard the garlic. Stir the butter and Parmesan into the rice and check the seasoning.

FISH

FISH

≋

The Romans called the Mediterranean *mare nostrum*, and Italy's long coastline means you are never far from the sea. Italians love fish and today, when local waters cannot satisfy the demand, costly cargoes are flown in from North Africa and the Atlantic and Pacific oceans. An Italian will very happily eat fish or seafood at every course if he is lucky enough to have the chance. Fish enhances any pasta or rice dish and when you gaze at the glistening, colorful catch at the Rialto fish market in Venice, or Porta Nolana in Naples, you long to start cooking.

Away from the Mediterranean it is sometimes difficult to find all the fish and shellfish used in these recipes. Do experiment with the choice available, and at times be content to substitute frozen shellfish. Alan Davidson's *Mediterranean Seafood*, published by Penguin, has long been my 'bible' on my travels – I have worn out two copies! It will always point you in the right direction.

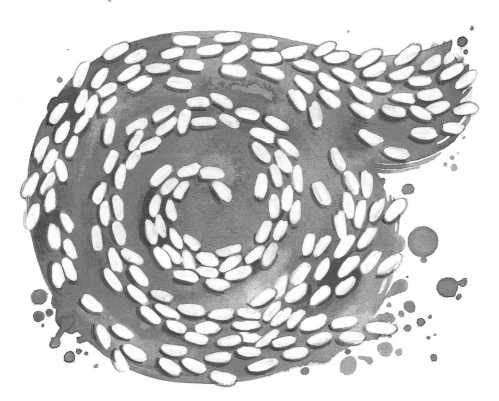

RISOTTO CON GAMBERI

Prawn Risotto

This is a comparatively easy seafood risotto that
can be made quite successfully with shelled or even frozen prawns
(shrimps), but you do need to use a good fish stock.

SERVES 4

125ml/4½ fl oz (generous ½ cup) dry white wine
1 bay leaf
salt and black pepper
200g/7 oz shelled prawns (shrimps)
2 tablespoons extra virgin olive oil
1 small onion, finely chopped
1 clove garlic, finely chopped
350g/12 oz (2 cups) Vialone nano rice (or Carnaroli or Arborio)
1 litre/1¾ pints (4 cups) good fish stock
1 tablespoon finely chopped fresh parsley

Put the wine and a cup or so of water in a pan with the bay leaf and a
little salt and bring to a boil. Add the prawns and cook for 5 minutes. If
the prawns are already cooked just plunge them in the boiling liquid and
take off the heat. Pour the cooking liquid through a strainer and keep for
the rice.

Heat the oil in a large pan and gently cook the onion and garlic until
soft. Stir in the rice and after 5 minutes stir in first the prawn liquid, a
little at a time, and then continue with the stock, adding more as it
becomes absorbed. When the rice is cooked but *al dente* – this takes 15 to
20 minutes – remove from the heat and stir in the parsley, prawns and a
little black pepper.

Cheese is not usually served with fish or shellfish risotto

RISO ALLA CERTOSINA

Rice with Vegetables and Shellfish

There are many versions of this traditional rice dish.
Originally it was made by the monks from the Charterhouse (la certosa)
at Pavia in the Po Valley, and its ingredients were influenced by their
religious rules and fast days. Since then other ingredients like butter,
fish fillets and frogs have crept into the dish, in a profusion that
would have shocked the abbot. This is the traditional recipe.

SERVES 4

2 tablespoons extra virgin olive oil
1 clove garlic, crushed with the back of a knife
200g/7 oz fresh mushrooms, sliced, or 20g/¾ oz dried porcini
200g/7 oz shelled peas
200ml/7 fl oz (1 cup) fresh tomato sauce (see page 15)
salt and black pepper
350g/12 oz crayfish (crawfish) or fresh water prawns (shrimps),
cleaned and shelled
350g/12 oz (2 cups) Carnaroli rice (or Vialone nano or Arborio)

Heat the oil in a pan and stir the garlic around in it until it begins to
change color, then discard. If you are using dried porcini, soak them for
10 minutes in warm water. Stir the mushrooms, peas and tomato sauce
into the pan, season to taste and simmer gently for 5 minutes.

In another pan bring 700ml/1¼ pints (3 cups) lightly salted water to
a boil and cook the shellfish for 5 minutes. Lift out with a slotted spoon
and strain the cooking water, return it to the pan and bring it back to a
boil. Add the rice and simmer for 10 minutes. Drain and stir in the
shellfish with the mushroom, peas and tomato sauce and serve.

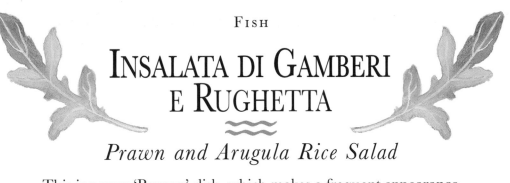

Insalata di Gamberi e Rughetta

Prawn and Arugula Rice Salad

This is a very 'Roman' dish, which makes a frequent appearance at large buffets for weddings and similar festivities. Many of the other 'imported' dishes at these events are usually smothered in heavy mayonnaise, so I always make straight for the fresh-tasting *Prawn and Arugula Rice Salad*.

Serves 4

3 tablespoons extra virgin olive oil
1 clove garlic
2cm fresh ginger root
300g/10½ oz prawns (shrimps),
shelled, de-veined and seasoned
1 tablespoon dry white wine
juice of 2 lemons
300g/10½ oz (1⅔ cups) Arborio rice (or Carnaroli or Vialone nano)
300g/10½ oz arugula, washed and any tough stalks removed
salt and black pepper

Heat 1 tablespoon of the oil in a pan and stir in the whole peeled garlic and ginger. Add the prawns, splash with the wine and stir for a few minutes. Remove the pan from the heat, lift the prawns out on to a plate, squeeze some lemon juice over and discard the garlic and ginger.

Bring 500ml/18 fl oz (2 cups) lightly salted water to a boil and simmer the rice for 15 to 20 minutes unitl cooked, adding more boiling water when it becomes dry. Drain and spread out on a large plate to cool. Mix together the rice and arugula in a salad bowl, check the seasoning and dress with the remaining lemon juice and olive oil. Arrange the prawns over the top and serve.

RISOTTO DI ZUCCHINI E GAMBERI

Zucchini and Prawn Risotto

Many of the top Italian restaurants favor the combination of zucchini and seafood. This recipe is a simplified version. It is essential to use young, firm zucchinis.

SERVES 4

350g/12 oz whole prawns (shrimps) or 200g/7 oz shelled
3 tablespoons extra virgin olive oil
200g/7 oz young zucchinis
1 small onion, finely chopped
350g/12 oz (2 cups) Carnaroli rice (or Vialone nano or Arborio)
1 litre/1¾ pints (4 cups) light meat or fish stock
salt and black pepper
1 tablespoon chopped fresh parsley

If you are using whole prawns remove heads and shell. Cut either type in half lengthwise and remove the vein. Heat half the oil and quickly cook the prawns. Remove and set aside.

Cut the zucchinis in quarters lengthwise and dice. In the same pan, heat the rest of the oil and cook the onion until soft. Stir in the zucchinis and after a few minutes add the rice. Cook, stirring, for 5 minutes then start adding the boiling stock, a ladle at a time, waiting for the rice to absorb the liquid before stirring in more. Continue to stir for 15 to 20 minutes and when the rice is cooked and the stock is absorbed, remove from the heat, check the seasoning and stir in the prawns and parsley.

RISOTTO AGLI SCAMPI

Dublin Bay Prawn Risotto

This recipe can be used with Dublin Bay prawns (scampi) or prawns (shrimps). In Venice the tiny lagoon shrimps are used and can be enjoyed at 'Fiore' restaurant. If you cannot find raw prawns or scampi I suggest you use the alternative recipe on page 49.

SERVES 4

350g/12 oz unshelled raw Dublin Bay prawns
(scampi) or prawns (shrimps)
salt and black pepper
2 cloves garlic, peeled
1 bay leaf
50g/2 oz (½ stick) butter
1 small onion or shallot, finely chopped
350g/12 oz (2 cups) Vialone nano rice (or Carnaroli or Arborio)
100ml/3½ fl oz (½ cup) dry white wine
1 tablespoon fresh tomato sauce (see page 15)

Remove the heads and shell from the scampi or prawns. To make the stock, wash the heads and shells and put them in a pan with 1.5 litres/2¾ pints (6 cups) water, salt, garlic and bay leaf. Bring to a boil and simmer for at least an hour. Strain the stock before starting to make the risotto.

Remove the central vein from the shellfish and set them to one side. Heat half the butter in a large pan and gently cook the onion or shallot until soft. Add the rice and stir around the pan for 5 minutes, then splash with the wine. Stir in the stock slowly a ladle at a time until no more liquid is absorbed (there will be stock left over). After 10 minutes stir in the tomato sauce and the scampi. Cook for a further 5 or 10 minutes until the rice is cooked, adjust seasoning and serve.

RISOTTO CON PEOICI ALLA VENETA

Venetian Mussel Risotto

This is a Venetian risotto cooked *all'onda*, so that it ripples like a wave on the plate. In the eighteenth century it used to be served at state banquets, and it is the forefather of *Risotto alla Marinara*, see page 60.

SERVES 4

1.5 kg/3 lb 5 oz mussels in their shells
100ml/3½ fl oz (½ cup) dry white wine
1 tablespoon finely chopped fresh parsley, reserving the stalks
1 litre/1¾ pints (4 cups) fish or light meat stock
salt and black pepper
3 tablespoons extra virgin olive oil
50g/2 oz (½ stick) butter
1 small onion, finely chopped
2 cloves garlic, crushed with the back of a knife
1 dried chile pepper
350g/12 oz (2 cups) Vialone nano rice (or Carnaroli or Arborio)

Scrape the mussels under running water, removing the 'beard' and discarding any open or broken shells. Put them in a covered pan with a little water, white wine and parsley stalks, and cook until the shells open. Discard any that fail to open. Drain the mussels, keeping several of the most attractive half shells with the mussels still attached for decoration and reserve the liquid. Shell the other mussels and chop unless they are very small. Pour the cooking liquid through a fine sieve, preferably lined with cheesecloth. Heat the stock and add the mussel liquid. Taste and adjust the seasoning.

Heat the oil and half the butter in a large pan. Add the onion, garlic and chile and cook gently until they begin to change color. Discard the chile and garlic. Add the rice and stir around in the pan for about 5 minutes. Do not let the rice change color. Start adding the stock a ladle at a time, stirring carefully until it is nearly absorbed. The rice will take about 20 minutes to cook, but keep tasting to be sure. The risotto should be runny and not be too dense. Stir in the chopped parsley, remaining butter and shelled mussels, grind black pepper over, top with mussels in half shells and serve at once.

55

Riso, Patate e Cozze

≈≈≈

Tiella with Rice, Mussels and Potato

The Spanish influence is seen clearly in these baked rice dishes from Puglia. In Bari this is called *Riso, Patate e Cozze,* while in Lecce it is named after the dish *tiella* in which it is cooked. It is one of the great Italian dishes, prepared superbly at the hotel 'Melograno' in Monopoli. Served in the huge terra-cotta dish and carried from table to table, it is impossible to resist second helpings. The *tiella* is lovingly wrapped in a thick cloth to keep it warm but it is best left to stand for a while after it has been removed from the oven, to savor the tastes and aroma as they combine. This version comes from Dr Camillo Guerra, genial host at the 'Melograno' and a noted *buongustaio.*

Serves 4

200g/7 oz (scant 1¼ cups) Arborio rice (or Carnaroli or Vialone nano)
1.5 kg /3 lb 5 oz mussels in their shells
4 tablespoons extra virgin olive oil
2 medium red onions, sliced
5 good sized waxy yellow potatoes, sliced
200g/7 oz small red tomatoes, peeled (see page 25) and halved
1 tablespoon finely chopped fresh parsley
salt and black pepper
100g/4 oz (1¼ cups) grated pecorino
3 cloves garlic, peeled and left for an hour in
4 tablespoons extra virgin olive oil

Preheat the oven to 180°C/350°F.

Soak the rice in 500ml/18 fl oz (2 cups) of cold water. Scrape the mussels under running water, removing the 'beard' and discarding any open or broken shells. If you are on the coast and the mussels are straight from the sea they can be opened as if they were oysters, their liquid carefully preserved and used raw as in Puglia. The rest of us have to content ourselves by letting them open quickly while cooking in a little boiling water. Discard any that fail to open. Drain and pour the mussel liquid through a fine sieve lined with cheesecloth if possible to remove any sand and set aside. Drain the rice reserving the water.

Put 2 tablespoons of the extra virgin olive oil into a large ovenproof dish, preferably terra-cotta. Arrange a thin layer of onion covered by a thin layer of potatoes over the bottom of the dish. Place 5 or 6 pieces of tomato on top and sprinkle with a little parsley and seasoning. Arrange a few mussels in their half shell over this, followed by a handful of wet rice and a sprinkling of pecorino. Drizzle on 2 tablespoons garlic flavored oil. Continue to build up the layers finishing with potato, tomato and pecorino.

Drizzle on the remaining 2 tablespoons olive oil and carefully pour the rice water down the sides of the prepared dish until the liquid reaches the top potato level. Use the mussel water if you need more water. Put the ovenproof dish on to a burner, using a heat diffuser if necessary, until it comes to a boil. Remove and bake in the oven for 40 minutes. Check after 30 minutes for dryness and dribble a little more liquid, or water if the rice and mussel water are finished, down the sides, if necessary.

Allow to rest for an hour or so before serving.

RISOTTO AI CALAMARI

Risotto with Squid

Variations of this dish can be found all round Italy's long coastline. Small baby *polpi* (octopus), or *seppioline* (cuttlefish) can be used instead of *calamari* (squid). Cheese is not usually served with seafood risotto.

SERVES 4

4 tablespoons extra virgin olive oil
1 clove garlic, finely chopped
1 onion, finely chopped
350g/12 oz squid, cleaned and cut into strips
400g/14 oz canned Italian plum tomatoes,
deseeded and chopped
2 teaspoons chopped fresh marjoram
salt and black pepper
350g/12 oz (2 cups) Carnaroli rice (or Vialone nano or Arborio)
1 litre/1¾ pints (4 cups) fish or vegetable stock
1 tablespoon finely chopped fresh parsley

Heat half the oil in a pan and cook the garlic and half the onion until they begin to change color. Add the squid, cover and cook gently for 10 minutes. Stir in the tomatoes, marjoram, salt and pepper. Cover and cook for a further 10 minutes. In another pan, heat the remaining oil and let the rest of the onion soften before stirring in the rice. Start to add the boiling stock a little at a time, waiting for the rice to absorb the liquid before stirring in more, and after 15 minutes when the rice is almost cooked *al dente* stir in the squid mixture and parsley. Cook for another few minutes then serve at once.

Riso con gli 'Angeli'

Sicilian Rice with Angels

The joined mussel shells could seem like angels' wings to a devout soul enjoying the heavenly flavors of Sicilian food, especially after a few glasses of crisp, chilled white wine! This dish can be cooked in advance and quickly reheated and assembled before the meal.

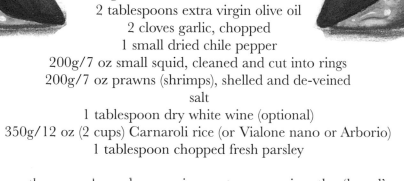

SERVES 4

500g/1 lb 2 oz mussels in their shells
2 tablespoons extra virgin olive oil
2 cloves garlic, chopped
1 small dried chile pepper
200g/7 oz small squid, cleaned and cut into rings
200g/7 oz prawns (shrimps), shelled and de-veined
salt
1 tablespoon dry white wine (optional)
350g/12 oz (2 cups) Carnaroli rice (or Vialone nano or Arborio)
1 tablespoon chopped fresh parsley

Scrape the mussels under running water, removing the 'beard' and discarding any open or broken shells. Put them in a covered pan with a little water and bring to a boil. Discard any mussels that fail to open. Drain and pour the cooking liquid through a fine sieve lined with cheese-cloth if possible and put to one side with the cooked, open mussels.

Heat the oil in a frying pan and gently cook the garlic until it begins to turn golden brown. Add the chile and stir in the squid. Cook gently until tender. Add the prawns and cook for a few minutes more. Season with a little salt and splash with the white wine. Let the wine evaporate then turn off the heat.

Check the salt level in the mussel liquid before bringing to a boil in a separate pan with enough water to cook the rice. Season with a little salt if necessary. Cook the rice gently uncovered for about 20 minutes until it is *al dente* when it should still have a little 'bite'. Drain the rice and stir in the parsley and shellfish.

RISOTTO ALLA MARINARA

Seafood Risotto

Italy has a long, long coastline and a myriad of fish dishes.
This risotto is created by Fulvio Pierangelini at his restaurant 'Gambero
Rosso' in San Vincenzo in Tuscany. The restaurant is on the sea front
and the fish is '*sa di mare*', as the Italians say when they want to praise
the fresh-out-of-the-sea taste. Fulvio uses a variety of seafood but if
you can't get cuttlefish increase the quantity of small squid, and you
can have more mussels to compensate for lack of clams.

SERVES 4

300g/10½ oz mussels in their shells
100g/4 oz clams in their shells
3 tablespoons extra virgin olive oil
1 onion, finely chopped
1 small piece dried chile
4 small squid (*moscardini*),cleaned and cut into strips
1 cuttlefish, cleaned and cut into strips
300g/10½ oz (1⅔ cups) Carnaroli rice (or Vialone nano or Arborio)
150ml/5 fl oz (⅔ cup) dry white wine
1 litre/1¾ pints (4 cups) fish stock made from prawn heads and shells
3 canned Italian plum tomatoes
1 tablespoon chopped fresh oregano (optional)
salt and black pepper
4 large prawns (shrimps), shelled and de-veined
1 tablespoon chopped fresh parsley
very good olive oil for drizzling (optional)

Scrape the mussels under running water, removing the 'beard' and clean
the clams. Discard any open or broken shells. Steam both the mussels and
the clams in a little boiling water until the shells open and discard any that
don't. Cool and remove from their shells.

Heat the oil in a large pan and gently cook the onion, chile, squid and
cuttlefish for 2 minutes. Stir in the rice, and cook, stirring around the pan,
for 5 minutes then pour in the wine. When it has evaporated, start adding
the boiling fish stock to the rice, ladle by ladle, stirring all the time. After
10 minutes add the mussels and clams and stir in the tomatoes and

oregano, if available. Check seasoning and continue to add a little more stock until the rice is cooked *al dente*.

Season the prawns and quickly cook them in a non-stick pan, on both sides, for 3 minutes. Stir the parsley into the risotto and serve with the prawns arranged over the top. Some people like to drizzle a little very good olive oil over the finished dish.

RISOTTO AL SALMONE AFFUMICATO

Smoked Salmon Risotto

Smoked salmon has now become an integral part of Italian festive fare, and this 'new' recipe is very popular with home cooks who want to make something easy but special. Fish stock is too strong for this dish, so it is better to use vegetable stock.

SERVES 4

50g/2 oz (½ stick) butter
100g/4 oz sliced smoked salmon, cut into small squares
2 tablespoons extra virgin olive oil
1 small onion, finely chopped
300g/10½ oz (1⅔ cups) Vialone nano rice (or Carnaroli or Arborio)
100ml/3½ fl oz (½ cup) dry white wine
1 litre/1¾ pints (4 cups) vegetable stock
salt and black pepper
1 tablespoon finely chopped fresh parsley or dill

Melt the butter in a pan and stir in the salmon. Put to one side. Heat the oil in another pan and gently cook the onion until soft. Add the rice and stir for a few minutes before adding the wine. When the wine has evaporated start adding the boiling stock a ladle at a time, waiting for the rice to absorb the liquid before stirring in more. When the rice is cooked, after about 15 to 20 minutes, stir in the melted butter and smoked salmon, check the seasoning and garnish with the fresh parsley or dill.

RISOTTO ALLE CAPESANTE

Risotto with Scallops

A 'new' recipe from the Adriatic. If your scallops have the coral attached be careful to leave it intact or it will stain the risotto orange.

SERVES 4

4 tablespoons extra virgin olive oil
1 onion, finely chopped
8 arugula leaves
100ml/3½ fl oz (½ cup) double (heavy) cream
8 scallops
salt and black pepper
100ml/3½ fl oz (½ cup) dry white wine
350g/12 oz (2 cups) Vialone nano rice (or Carnaroli or Arborio)
1 litre/1¾ pints (4 cups) fish or light meat stock

Heat half the oil in a pan and gently cook half the onion until soft. Add the arugula leaves and cream, then cook, stirring, until the mixture thickens. Blend or process and set aside.

Remove the scallops from their shells if necessary and clean. Slice the white part, leaving the coral intact and season. In another pan heat the white wine and gently cook the scallops for a few minutes. Lift out with a slotted spoon, set aside and reserve the cooking liquid. Heat the remaining oil in a large pan and cook the rest of the onion until soft. Stir in the rice and after 5 minutes stir in the scallop liquid. Keep stirring while adding the stock a little at a time, until the rice is cooked. This should take about 15 to 20 minutes. Stir in the cream and scallops and serve at once.

RISO AL SALMONE

Rice with Salmon

Now that salmon has become so easily available, it is used
in many guises. Here it is combined with rice to make a
delicately flavored one-dish meal.

SERVES 4

300g/10½ oz (1⅔ cups) Carnaroli rice (or Vialone nano or Arborio)
2 tablespoons extra virgin olive oil
1 clove garlic, crushed with the back of a knife
200g/7 oz salmon, skinned, boned and diced
100ml/3½ fl oz (½ cup) dry white wine
250ml/9 fl oz (1¼ cups) vegetable or fish stock
1 tablespoon chopped fresh chives
salt and black pepper

Cook the rice in a large pan of boiling, salted water (see page 4). Drain.
Heat the oil in another pan and add the garlic. When it begins to change
color discard it. Add the salmon and stir gently before splashing with the
wine. When the wine has evaporated add the stock, bring to a boil, cover
and simmer for 10 minutes. Remove from the heat and stir in the rice.
Garnish with chives, season with black pepper and serve at once.

RISOTTO ALLA CHIOGGIOTTA

Risotto with Fish from the Lagoon

This traditional fish risotto gets its name from the Venetian fishing port, Chioggia. The fish used in Venice are small bony fish from the lagoon, known as *go* or *ghiozzi*. This is one of the few Italian fish dishes that requires Parmesan cheese at the end. There are some purists who refuse to accept this exception!

SERVES 4

2 tablespoons extra virgin olive oil
80g/3 oz (¾ stick) butter
1 small onion, finely chopped
1 clove garlic, chopped
500g/1 lb 2 oz small, whole, non-oily fish suitable for soup
salt and black pepper
350g/12 oz (2 cups) Vialone nano rice (or Carnaroli or Arborio)
150ml/5 fl oz (¾ cup) dry white wine
1 tablespoon chopped fresh parsley
30g/1 oz (⅓ cup) freshly grated Parmesan (optional)

Heat the oil and half the butter in a large pan and gently fry the onion and garlic until soft. Add the whole fish, salt and pepper. Cook for 2 minutes on each side and then add about 250ml/9 fl oz (1¼ cups) of cold water, cover and simmer for 15 minutes. Lift out the fish, remove the skin and central bone, and pass it through a food mill, adding some of the cooking liquid if it makes the process easier. This part of the recipe can be prepared in advance and stored in the fridge.

When ready to eat bring a large pan of water to a boil and keep it simmering on a back burner for the risotto. Heat the remaining butter in another pan and add a little of the fish purée. When it begins to bubble stir in the rice and after a few minutes pour over the white wine. When this has evaporated gradually add the rest of the fish purée, stirring all the time. When the purée has been absorbed by the rice, add one ladle of boiling water at a time until the risotto is *al dente*. Take off the heat, check the seasoning, then sprinkle with parsley. Parmesan can be handed round separately at table.

INSALATA DI RISO AI FRUTTI DI MARE

Seafood Rice Salad

This salad can be made with any shellfish. It makes a refreshing summer starter or buffet party dish.

SERVES 4

500g/1 lb 2 oz mussels in their shells
100ml/3½ fl oz (½ cup) white wine vinegar
1 bay leaf
2 small octopus if available, cleaned and sliced
200g/7 oz shelled prawns (shrimps)
salt and black pepper
350g/12 oz (2 cups) Carnaroli rice (or Vialone nano or Arborio)
juice of 1 lemon
4 tablespoons extra virgin olive oil
1 tablespoon chopped fresh parsley

Scrape the mussels under running water, removing the 'beard' and discarding any open or broken shells. Put them in a pan with a little water and bring to a boil. Discard any that fail to open. Remove the mussels from their shells and place them in a large salad bowl. Bring some lightly salted water to a boil with the vinegar and bay leaf. Add the octopus and simmer until tender. Remove and place with the mussels. Cook the prawns in the same water for 3 minutes. Lift out and place with the other shellfish. Season to taste.

In another pan bring 700ml/1¼ pints (3 cups) lightly salted water to a boil, add the rice and simmer for 15 minutes. Drain if necessary and spread the rice out on a plate to cool. Add to the shellfish and stir in the lemon juice, olive oil and parsley.

RISOTTO NERO CON LE SEPPIE

Black Risotto with Cuttlefish Ink

This traditional Venetian dish has become very trendy outside Italy, but I usually wait until I am in Venice lunching at 'Da Fiore', my favorite Venetian restaurant in San Polo, to indulge.

SERVES 4

2 tablespoons extra virgin olive oil
1 clove garlic, finely chopped
1 small onion, finely chopped
2 tablespoons finely chopped fresh parsley
500g/1 lb 2 oz small cuttlefish, cleaned and cut into strips (ink sac intact)
100ml/3½ fl oz (½ cup) dry white wine
300g/10½ oz (1⅔ cups) Vialone nano rice (or Carnaroli or Arborio)
1 litre/1¾ pints (4 cups) light meat or fish stock
salt and black pepper

Heat the oil in a large pan and gently cook the garlic and onion until soft. Stir in the parsley and cuttlefish then splash with white wine. Break 2 of the ink sacs into the pan – they can easily be squashed between 2 spoons to avoid a mess – and continue to cook. After 10 minutes stir in the rice and when it has absorbed some of the flavors gradually start adding the boiling stock, ladle by ladle, waiting for the rice to absorb the liquid before stirring in more. It will take about 15 to 20 minutes to cook when it should be *all'onda*. Adjust the seasoning and serve.

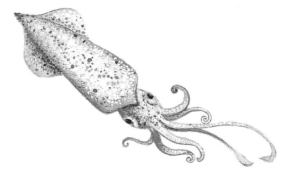

RISOTTO AL TONNO

Tuna Risotto

This is an easy risotto but you do need to use good tuna, preferably canned in olive oil. The Arabic influence in Sicilian cooking is shown in the frequent use of mint which adds an interesting note.

SERVES 4

2 tablespoons extra virgin olive oil
1 onion, finely chopped
1 clove garlic, finely chopped
350g/12 oz (2 cups) Carnaroli rice (or Vialone nano or Arborio)
150g/5½ oz canned Italian plum tomatoes, chopped
salt and black pepper
1.2 litres/2 pints (5 cups) light meat stock
100g/3½ oz canned tuna in oil, drained and flaked
6 mint leaves, chopped

Heat the olive oil in a large pan and gently cook the onion and garlic until soft. Stir in the rice and after 5 minutes add the tomatoes, salt and pepper. Stir around the pan then start adding the stock a ladle at a time, waiting for the rice to absorb the liquid before stirring in more. After 15 to 20 minutes, when the rice is cooked but *al dente*, remove from the heat and stir in the tuna and mint. Serve at once.

Riso al Tonno

Rice with Sun-dried Tomatoes and Tuna

If you don't like dealing with whole fish this easy rice dish will appeal to you. It is a good way of using the fresh tuna left over after a cutlet has been trimmed to make a symmetrical steak.

Serves 4

4 tablespoons extra virgin olive oil
2 cloves garlic, chopped
2 sun-dried tomatoes in olive oil, chopped
8 black olives, pitted and chopped
1 tablespoon chopped fresh parsley
500g/1 lb 2 oz fresh tuna, cubed
75ml/2½ fl oz (⅓ cup) dry white wine
salt and black pepper
350g/12 oz (2 cups) Carnaroli rice (or Vialone nano or Arborio)
1 onion, finely chopped

Heat half the oil in a pan and gently cook the garlic, tomatoes, olives and parsley for a few minutes. Stir in the cubes of tuna and cook for 5 minutes. Pour over the wine, season, cover and leave to stand.

Bring 700ml/1¼ pints (3 cups) lightly salted water to a boil in a large saucepan and cook the rice for about 15 minutes. Heat the remaining oil in another pan and cook the onion until soft. Drain the rice and stir into the onion. Cook for 3 to 4 minutes more then stir in the tuna mixture and serve.

MINESTRA DI RISO E PESCE

Rice and Fish Broth

In the Abruzzo, on the Adriatic coast, this *minestra* is made
with pasta or rice. You can decide whether you want to serve it as
a *primo piatto* (starter) or a one-dish meal. If you choose to make a meal
of it, use more fish, which should be kept in larger fillets and served
at the bottom of the soup plate, with the *minestra* on top.

SERVES 4

4 tablespoons extra virgin olive oil
2 cloves garlic, finely chopped
½ dried chile, crumbled
450g/1 lb canned Italian plum tomatoes,
deseeded and chopped
a whole white fish, weighing about 800g/1 lb 12 oz, cleaned
and scaled, or 4 fillets
1 tablespoon finely chopped fresh parsley
100ml/3½ fl oz (½ cup) dry white wine
salt and black pepper
250g/9 oz (scant 1½ cups) Carnaroli rice
(or Vialone nano or Arborio)
1 handful arugula, chopped

Heat the oil in a large pan and stir in the garlic. As it begins to change
color, add the chile and tomatoes. Cook for 5 minutes then put in
the fish, parsley, wine and 500ml/18 fl oz (2 cups) water. Sprinkle in a
little salt, bring to a boil, cover and poach for 30 minutes, if using
a whole fish, 15 minutes for fillets. Carefully lift out the fish, without
breaking if possible. Skin and fillet the whole fish and cut the fillets into
pieces about 1 1/2 inches long and leave in a warm place.

Bring the cooking liquid back to a boil and pour in the rice. Simmer
gently for 15 to 20 minutes, adding a little more boiling water when
necessary. When the rice is cooked it should still be very liquid because
this is a *minestra* which is eaten with a spoon. Check the seasoning. Pour a
little of the boiling liquid over the fish then with a slotted spoon put half
the pieces in individual soup plates. Ladle on the rice and tomato broth,
a little arugula and the rest of the fish.

Riso con Pesce Persico

Rice with Fried Fish Fillets

At Lake Como this is made with fillets of perch,
but it is equally good with any fresh or salt-water fish.

Serves 4

150g/5½ oz (1¼ sticks) butter
400g/14 oz (2⅓ cups) Carnaroli rice (or Vialone nano or Arborio)
100ml/3½ fl oz (½ cup) dry white wine
700ml/1¼ pints (3 cups) light meat stock
1 onion, peeled and left whole
300g/10½ oz fish fillets
plain (all-purpose) white flour for dredging
salt
1 egg, beaten
2 sage leaves

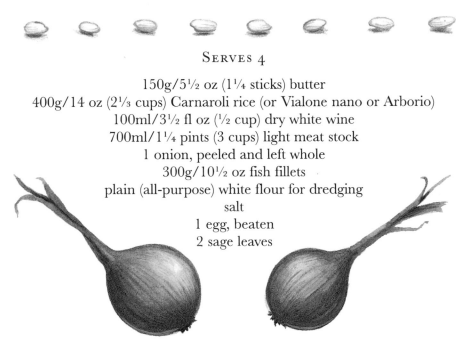

Heat 50g/2 oz (½ stick) of the butter in a large pan and stir the rice around in it for 5 minutes. Pour on the wine and keep stirring until it has evaporated, then add the stock and the whole onion. Cover and cook gently for 15 minutes.

Lightly dredge the fish with flour, season and dip in the egg and in another pan fry the fillets in half the remaining butter. Add the sage when you turn the fish over to cook the second side.

Remove the onion from the rice and run a fork through it to separate the grains. Serve the rice with the fried fish on top.

MEAT
AND
POULTRY

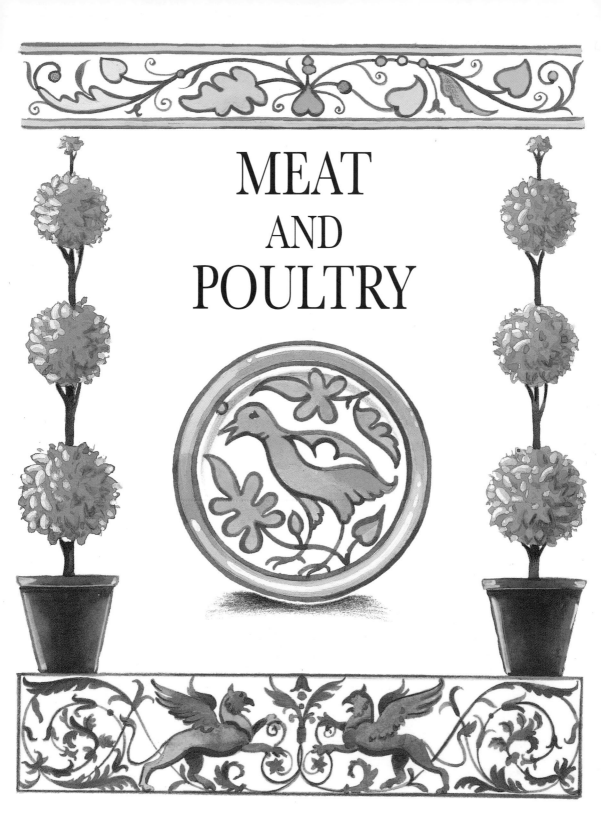

MEAT AND POULTRY

Meat does not play a dominant role in Italian cooking since, like most Mediterranean countries, Italy does not have the climate for lush pasture-lands. In the past when Italy was a comparatively poor country, most people could not afford to eat meat very often and they found ingenious ways to make several meals from one piece of meat. For this reason Italian rice dishes with meat are often elaborate and time-consuming, intended for celebrations and special occasions. Many households used to keep a pig, feeding it on kitchen scraps and whatever came to hand, so pork, sausages and bacon are often used to give substance and robust flavor to one-dish rice meals.

Traditionally, every family used to keep its own poultry and even today *cortile* or courtyard chicken, are reared for the table. This probably explains why guinea fowl, duck and even pigeon are treated with more ceremony.

RISOTTO ALLA PITOCCA

Chicken Risotto from Lombardy

This is a speciality from Brescia in northern Italy. *Pitocca* means
'not rich' so you should carefully remove the fat from the chicken
before cooking. Although it is simpler to use boned chicken,
the bones do give extra flavor to the risotto.

SERVES 4

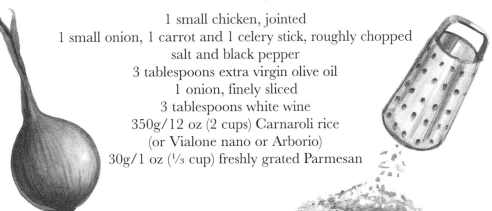

1 small chicken, jointed
1 small onion, 1 carrot and 1 celery stick, roughly chopped
salt and black pepper
3 tablespoons extra virgin olive oil
1 onion, finely sliced
3 tablespoons white wine
350g/12 oz (2 cups) Carnaroli rice
(or Vialone nano or Arborio)
30g/1 oz (1/3 cup) freshly grated Parmesan

Trim the chicken pieces, putting the breast and legs to one side. To make
the stock, remove any visible fat from the remaining pieces and put them
into a large pan with the roughly chopped onion, carrot and celery.
Season, cover with water, bring to a boil and simmer for at least an hour.

Chop the breast and legs into small pieces. Heat the oil in another pan
and let the sliced onion soften before adding the chicken pieces to brown.
Season and add the wine. Cook until the meat can be removed from the
bone, then return it to the pan and stir in the rice. Stir around the pan for
4 minutes then start gradually adding the drained, boiling chicken stock.
Add the stock a ladle at a time, waiting for the rice to absorb the liquid
before stirring in more. Continue until the rice is cooked after about 20
minutes when it should be *al dente*. Serve at once. Parmesan can be passed
round at table if desired.

ZUPPA DI POLLO CON RISO

Chicken and Rice Soup

The old ghetto in Venice is a tranquil haven after St Mark's Square.
And this is where I feel the origins of this simple soup lie, lovingly
made by generations of Venetian mothers to comfort,
soothe and delight their families.

SERVES 4

30g/1 oz (¼ stick) butter
2 tablespoons extra virgin olive oil
1 onion, finely chopped
1 tablespoon freshly chopped parsley
1 sage leaf, chopped
200g/7 oz chicken breast, cubed
1 litre/1¾ pints (4 cups) light meat (chicken) stock
1 tablespoon fresh tomato sauce (see page 15)
salt and black pepper
200g/7 oz (scant 1¼ cups) Vialone nano rice (or Carnaroli or Arborio)
50g/2 oz (generous ½ cup) freshly grated Parmesan (optional)

Heat half the butter and the oil in a large pan and gently cook the onion
and herbs. Stir in the chicken and cook for a few minutes before adding
half the stock, the tomato sauce and seasoning. Cover and cook gently
for 30 minutes. Add the rest of the stock, bring to a boil and pour in
the rice. Simmer for 15 minutes, then stir in the remaining butter and
1 tablespoon of the Parmesan. Check the seasoning. Serve the remaining
cheese at table.

RISOTTO ALLA SBIRRAGLIA

Chicken and Veal Risotto

When the Veneto region was under Hapsburg rule, the Austrians were so enthusiastic about this speciality from Treviso that the locals cynically renamed it 'police informers' risotto'. The finished dish should ripple *all'onda* if the plate is tilted.

SERVES 4

1 small chicken
2 carrots, 2 celery sticks and 2 onions, finely chopped
salt and black pepper
50g/2 oz (½ stick) butter
100g/4 oz lean veal, cubed
2 tablespoons white wine
2 teaspoons fresh thyme
300g/10½ oz (1⅔ cups) Vialone nano rice
(or Carnaroli or Arborio)
30g/1 oz (⅓ cup) freshly grated
Parmesan (optional)

Remove the breast and leg meat from the chicken and cube. To make the stock put the chicken carcass in a pot with half the carrot, celery, onion and seasoning. Cover with cold water, bring to a boil and simmer for at least an hour.

Heat the butter in a large pan and stir in the chicken and veal. Season and pour on the wine. Cover and cook gently for 15 minutes. Stir in the remaining carrot, celery, onion and the thyme and cook for 5 minutes before adding the rice. Stir the rice around the pan then gradually add the drained, boiling chicken stock, a ladle at a time, waiting for the rice to absorb the liquid before stirring in more. When the risotto is cooked serve at once. Parmesan can be handed round at table.

RISOTTO CON TACCHINA

Turkey Risotto

In Lombardy there are several 'complete meal' rice dishes, and turkey will please all the family. If you are tempted to use up the Christmas bird make a good stock with the bones, some dark meat and the vegetables. Pour through a strainer, discarding the meat, and cut some fresh white and brown meat to reheat for a few minutes before serving with the risotto.

SERVES 4

500g/1 lb 2 oz raw turkey meat, cut into small pieces,
or 1 leg and some breast
1 carrot, 1 celery stick and 1 onion, roughly chopped
100ml/4 fl oz (½ cup) dry white wine
3 cloves
1 bay leaf
salt and black pepper
30g/1 oz (¼ stick) butter
1 onion, finely chopped
350g/12 oz (2 cups) Carnaroli rice (or Vialone nano or Arborio)
50g/2 oz (generous ½ cup) freshly grated Parmesan

Heat 2 litres/3½ pints (8 cups) water in a large pan and add the raw turkey, roughly chopped vegetables, white wine, cloves, bay leaf and seasoning. Bring to a boil and simmer for at least an hour or until the turkey is tender. Using a slotted spoon lift out the turkey and place in a bowl with some of the stock. Cover and put to one side. Pour the remaining stock through a sieve. This can all be prepared in advance.

Heat half the butter in a large pan and gently cook the finely chopped onion until soft. Add the rice and stir around the pan before pouring on the boiling stock a ladle at a time, waiting for the rice to absorb the liquid before adding more. Continue stirring for 15 to 20 minutes until the rice is cooked *al dente*. Meanwhile, gently reheat the turkey meat in a separate pan. Stir the Parmesan into the rice with the remaining butter and some black pepper. Place on a serving dish with the turkey arranged over the top.

RISOTTO ALL'ANATRA SELVATICA

Wild Duck Risotto

Wild ducks can be found in Emilia-Romagna and the
Veneto in the Po Valley, and there are various local dishes designed
to make the best of these somewhat scrawny birds. One year, the
'Locanda Cipriani' in Torcello stayed open all winter to accommodate
Ernest Hemingway who wanted to shoot wild duck while he worked
on a book. I only hope they made lots of risotto! The recipe
works equally well with other game birds.

SERVES 4

4 tablespoons extra virgin olive oil
1 clove garlic, minced
1kg/2 lb 2 oz duck, cut into small pieces
3 sage leaves
salt and black pepper
100ml/3½ fl oz (½ cup) dry white wine
200g/7 oz ripe tomatoes, skinned, deseeded (see page 25) and quartered
40g/1½ oz (⅓ stick) butter
1 onion, finely chopped
350g/12 oz (2 cups) Vialone nano rice (or Carnaroli or Arborio)
1 litre/1¾ pints (4 cups) rich meat stock
50g/2 oz (generous ½ cup) freshly grated Parmesan

Heat 2 tablespoons of the olive oil in a large pan and stir in the garlic,
duck, sage leaves and seasoning. Brown the duck on all sides then add
the wine and simmer until it has nearly evaporated. Stir in the
tomatoes, cover and cook gently for 30 minutes, adding a little hot water
if necessary.

Meanwhile, heat half the butter and the remaining oil in another pan.
Cook the onion until soft, then add the rice and stir around the pan for 5
minutes. Pour in the boiling stock a ladle at a time, waiting for the liquid
to be absorbed before stirring in more. After 10 minutes stir in a little of
the duck and pan juices to flavor the rice. When the rice is cooked stir in
the Parmesan and remaining butter. The duck should be handed round
separately and spooned on to the risotto.

RISO IN BRODO CON LA SALSICCIA

Rice and Sausage Broth

I make this very easy *minestra* from northern Italy for instant comfort in the colder months. It is essential to use good quality sausage. *Luganega* sausage is lean and full of flavor. It is usually red in color because wine is used in the making. It is sold in a thin, long glistening coil, not divided into links.

SERVES 4

approx. 1.2 litres/2 pints (5 cups) light meat stock,
plus 200ml/7 fl oz (1 cup) dry white wine
200g/7 oz very lean Italian sausage, *luganega* if available
200g/7 oz (scant 1¼ cups) Carnaroli rice (or Vialone nano or Arborio)
4 tablespoons freshly grated Parmesan
salt and black pepper
1 tablespoon finely chopped fresh parsley (optional)

Bring the stock and wine to a boil in a pan. Place the sausage on a board and remove the skin. Draw the prongs of the fork through the sausage to break up into very small fragments. Put the sausage into another large pan, pour over half the stock and bring it to a boil, taking care to avoid the pieces sticking together. Gradually add the rice. I usually alternate a little sausage with a little rice. Cover and simmer gently for about 25 minutes, adding more stock as necessary. The *minestra* should be thick but liquid. Remove from the heat, stir in the Parmesan, adjust the seasoning and serve.

If you wish you can serve it garnished with parsley for visual appeal, but it is not traditional.

Panissa

≈≈

Bean, Sausage and Bacon Risotto

Vercelli in the north-west is the center of rice production in Italy. The landscape shimmers with great flooded paddy fields and the quiet is broken by the insistent croak of the frogs who thrive in the wet terrain. *Panissa* is a speciality of Vercelli, similar to the *Paniscia* of neighboring Novara, and it can be enjoyed at the welcoming 'Il Paiolo' restaurant in Vercelli or 'Osteria Cascina dei Fiori' in Borgo Vercelli. Traditionally *salame d'la duja*, salami preserved in fat which keeps it soft, is used for this dish. It is better to substitute fresh sausage rather than hard, matured salami.

Serves 4

150g/5½ oz dried borlotti beans
100g/4 oz bacon
30g/1 oz (¼ stick) butter
2 onions, finely chopped
50g/2 oz fresh salami or good Italian meat sausage, sliced and broken up
350g/12 oz (2 cups) Carnaroli rice (or Vialone nano or Arborio)
100ml/3½ fl oz (½ cup) Barbera or other dry red wine
black pepper
1.5 litres/2¾ pints (6 cups) rich meat stock

Soak the beans in plenty of cold water for at least 12 hours. Remove the bacon rind and cook it with the beans in 500ml/18 fl oz (2 cups) water until the beans are soft. This usually takes an hour. Chop the bacon. Heat the butter in a large pan and add the onions, bacon and sausage. When the onion is really soft, stir in the rice and after 5 minutes add the wine. Simmer until it evaporates, then add some pepper and 500ml/18 fl oz (2 cups) of the stock. Cook for 15 to 20 minutes, stirring frequently and adding more stock to keep it from drying out. The finished dish should be moist but all the liquid should have been absorbed.

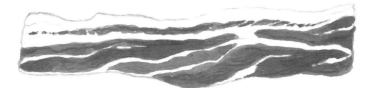

Risotto alla Pilòta

Rice Huskers' Risotto

The men who used to husk the rice were called *pilarini* or *pilòti* and they were entrusted with cooking the rice dishes for the rice workers. They had to be good. Today husking is done with machines but the name and tradition live on. There are several different recipes and this is the 'every day' version from Mantova, while *Riso col Puntel* (see page 85) was used to celebrate after a successful rice harvest. The different way of cooking the rice makes the rice grains dry and separate like a pilaf rice.

Serves 4

50g/2 oz (½ stick) butter
1 onion, finely chopped
300g/10½ oz lean pork, cubed
salt and black pepper
350g/12 oz (2 cups) Vialone nano rice (or Carnaroli or Arborio)
50g/2 oz (generous ½ cup) freshly grated Parmesan

Heat half the butter in a large pan and fry the onion until it begins to change color. Brown the pork, season and add a little water. Cover and cook until the pork is tender. Keep warm and cook the rice.

According to local lore to make a good *pilòta* you need the same quantity of rice and water plus half a cup of water for the pot. So far so good. Now it gets a bit obscure. Bring the water to a boil in a pan and pour the rice through a funnel into the middle to make a pyramid. The tip of the pyramid should appear just above the water. Now shake the pan so that the pyramid collapses. Add a little salt.

At this point let me be a heretic and say I omit all this pyramid business and it still works! Cover and simmer for 10 minutes on a fairly high heat, then remove the lid, cover with a folded tea towel, replace the lid and leave it to stand for 10 minutes to complete the cooking. Stir in the Parmesan, remaining butter and the pork mixture.

RISOTTO CON PANCETTA E CIPOLLE

Bacon and Onion Risotto

In Mantova the lake causes chilly, misty
autumn evenings, and this risotto
is the perfect antidote.

SERVES 4

30g/1 oz (¼ stick) butter
100g/4 oz bacon, chopped
1 large onion, chopped
350g/12 oz (2 cups) Vialone nano rice (or Carnaroli or Arborio)
150ml/5 fl oz (⅔ cup) full-bodied dry red wine
1 litre/1¾ pints (4 cups) rich meat stock
50g/2 oz (generous ½ cup) freshly grated Parmesan
black pepper

Melt the butter in a large pan and cook the bacon and onion until the
onion starts to color. Add the rice, stir around the pan for 5 minutes and
pour on the wine. Let it evaporate then start adding the boiling stock a
ladle at a time, waiting for the liquid to be absorbed before stirring in
more. After 15 to 20 minutes the risotto will be cooked *al dente*. Remove
from the heat and stir in the Parmesan and freshly ground black pepper.
Serve at once.

RISO ALLA GENOVESE

≈≈≈

Rice with Genovese Sauce

Genovese is the adjective of the city *Genova* (Genoa), but the sauce
for this dish comes from Naples and is unknown in Genoa. It is thought
to have been introduced into Naples in the fifteenth century by the
Genovese merchants who settled there and it became part of the
Neapolitan culinary tradition, although it was forgotten in Genoa
itself. It also seems to be related to several French dishes.
The Genovese sauce is served with pasta as well as rice, and
makes a sumptuous one-dish meal. In less affluent times the meat
would have been kept for another meal. I usually serve slices of the
meat with the Genovese rice or pasta but it can also be layered
up to make a *timballo* and baked in the oven in the same way
as the Sicilian *Tummàla* (see page 120).

SERVES 6

Genovese Sauce
4 tablespoons extra virgin
olive oil
1 carrot, finely chopped
1 stick celery, finely chopped
100g/4 oz prosciutto or bacon, finely chopped
1kg/2 lb 4 oz lean beef, preferably topside, tied to keep in shape
2kg/4 lb 8 oz onions, finely sliced
salt and black pepper

500g/1 lb 2 oz (3 cups) Carnaroli rice (or Vialone nano or Arborio)
100g/4 oz (1¼ cups) freshly grated Parmesan
salt and black pepper

The Genovese sauce takes about 2 hours to cook, but it can be prepared
the day before if preferred. Heat the oil in a pan and slowly cook the
carrot, celery and prosciutto or bacon. Add the beef and turn around in
the oil and vegetables browning on all sides. Transfer to a saucepan just
big enough to contain the meat covered with all the onions. Season, add
a little water, cover and bring to a boil. Turn the heat very low and keep
adding just enough water to stop the pan from drying out. This process is
called the *tirata* as the flavors are 'pulled out' of the meat. Scrape the

bottom of the pan from time to time with a wooden spoon. After 2 hours the sauce will be a rich chestnut color. Leave the meat to cool in the sauce and take it out and slice when you are ready to add the Genovese sauce to the rice.

To cook the rice bring 1 litre/1¾ pints (4 cups) lightly salted water to a boil in a pan and simmer for 10 minutes. Drain and stir in a little of the heated Genovese sauce, adding a spoonful at a time until the rice is cooked. Take off the heat, stir in the Parmesan and check the seasoning. Serve with the sliced meat and extra sauce handed round separately.

Riso col Puntel

Rice with Pork Chops

This is the rice harvest version of *Risotto alla Pilòta* (see page 81). When this used to be served in huge quantities for the rice workers it looked like a crown.

Serves 4

350g/12 oz (2 cups) Vialone nano rice (or Carnaroli or Arborio)
50g/2 oz (½ stick) butter
1 onion, finely chopped
4 pork chops
50g/2 oz (generous ½ cup) freshly grated Parmesan
salt and black pepper

Cook the rice *alla pilòta* (see page 81). Heat the butter and gently cook the onion until it begins to change color. Grill or barbecue the pork chops. When the rice is cooked, stir in the onion and Parmesan and check the seasoning. Serve on a large plate in a mound. Arrange the pork chops standing around the dish with the meat end on top, pointing outwards like a handle or *puntel*.

Riso in Tortiera

Baked Rice from Calabria

This is a very useful dish because it can be prepared in advance and put in the oven at the last minute when you get home or guests arrive. I have not been able to trace its origin but the hard-boiled eggs make me think that it could have been a party piece for *Carnevale* when eggs had to be used up before Lent.

Serves 4

2 tablespoons extra virgin olive oil
1 onion, finely chopped
250g/9 oz piece lean beef
100ml/4 fl oz (½ cup) dry red wine
6 basil leaves, roughly torn
500g/1 lb 2 oz canned Italian plum tomatoes
2 tablespoons fresh tomato sauce (see page 15)
1 egg, beaten
4 tablespoons fresh soft breadcrumbs
oil for frying
500g/1 lb 2 oz (3 cups) Carnaroli rice (or Vialone nano or Arborio)
3 hard-boiled (hardcooked) eggs, sliced (optional)
200g/7 oz mozzarella, sliced
100g/4 oz (1¼ cups) freshly grated pecorino
salt and black pepper

Preheat the oven to 200°C/400°F.

Heat the oil in a large pan and cook the onion until soft. Put in the meat and brown on all sides before pouring over the wine. Continue cooking until the wine has evaporated, then stir in the basil, the tomatoes and tomato sauce, squashing the tomatoes with the back of a wooden spoon to make a *ragù* (sauce). Add a little hot water, bring to a boil, cover and simmer until the meat is tender.

Lift out the cooked meat, reserving the *ragù*, and cut half of it into large chunks. Place the other half in a food processor with the beaten egg and 1 tablespoon of the fresh breadcrumbs. Blend to a smooth mixture and roll into tiny meatballs the size of a hazelnut. Fry in hot oil in another pan until golden brown, drain on a paper towel and keep to one side.

Meanwhile boil a large pan of lightly salted water and pour in the rice. Simmer until *al dente*, then drain and stir in three quarters of the *ragù*. Lightly oil a large ovenproof dish and sprinkle half the remaining breadcrumbs on the bottom. Make a flat layer of half the rice on top and cover with half the meatballs, pieces of meat, hard-boiled eggs, if using, mozzarella, the remaining *ragù*, pecorino and seasoning. Repeat these layers, finishing with the pecorino. Sprinkle over the remaining bread-crumbs and bake for 15 minutes to make a golden crust.

RISOTTO ALLA MILANESE

Milanese Risotto

Saffron is not a common ingredient in Lombardy cuisine, so there are many stories about the origins of this classic risotto. The ruling Sforza family used to give sumptuous feasts, decorating the finished dishes with gold leaf, and it is believed that other 'golden' dishes were invented to give the same feeling of opulence.

Another explanation is that the stained-glass *maestro*, employed to work on Sant' Elena's chapel in the Duomo in Milan, had an apprentice nicknamed 'Zafferano', or 'Saffron' who made liberal use of saffron to color his glass. Since he was mocked for this obsessive use of saffron, he persuaded the cook to make a saffron risotto for his patron's family wedding.

Today the controversial ingredient would be the marrow bone, which might ring alarm bells for the health-conscious. However it is not essential. Many versions use the juices left in the pan after meat has been roasted to give a rich flavor, and cooks in the town of Brescia add a judicious glass of good red wine. It is important to use a good beef stock. *Ossobuco* (see below), made from veal shins, is often served with the risotto. This introduces the bone marrow in another guise.

If you would like a dish fit for royalty, you can buy a little gold leaf from an art supplies shop or an Indian grocer and arrange a small piece on top of each serving of risotto.

SERVES 4

100g/4 oz (1 stick) butter or 50g/2 oz (½ stick) butter and
50ml/2 fl oz (¼ cup) fresh double (heavy) cream
1 onion, finely chopped
50g/2 oz bone marrow or roasting pan juices,
or 100ml/3½ fl oz (½ cup) dry red wine
350g/12 oz (2 cups) Carnaroli rice (or Vialone nano or Arborio)
1 litre/1¾ pints (4 cups) good beef stock
2 teaspoons saffron filaments, soaked in warm stock and drained
75g/2¾ oz (scant 1 cup) freshly grated Parmesan
black pepper

Ossobuco
1 tablespoon finely chopped fresh parsley
zest of 1 lemon
2 cloves garlic, minced or 1 anchovy fillet, minced
30g/1 oz (¼ stick) butter
1 onion, finely chopped
2 tablespoons extra virgin olive oil
4 portions of veal shins, lightly floured
150ml/5 fl oz (⅔ cup) dry white wine
4 tomatoes, peeled, deseeded (see page 25) and chopped
salt and black pepper

Heat half the butter in a large pan and gently cook the onion until soft. Add the bone marrow or pan juices if you are using them. Some people prefer to add them later. Add the rice and stir for 5 minutes. If you are using wine, pour over the rice, stirring slowly all the time before continuing with the stock, ladle by ladle. The rice will take about 20 minutes to cook, when each grain of rice should still be quite separate. About 5 minutes before the end of cooking time, add the saffron and the pan juices if not used already. Remove from the heat and stir in the remaining butter or cream and half the Parmesan. Add black pepper and serve at once with the rest of the cheese.

For the *Ossobuco*, mix together the parsley, lemon zest and either garlic or anchovy in a bowl to make a *gremolata* and set aside.

Melt the butter in a pan and gently cook the onion until soft. In another pan, heat the oil and lightly brown the meat on both sides. Cover with the onion and add the wine. After a few minutes stir in the tomatoes and salt and pepper, then cover and cook gently for 1½ hours. Add a little left over stock from time to time if the pan is getting too dry.

When ready to serve, lift the meat out with a slotted spoon, and either place it on top of the risotto with some *gremolata* sprinkled on top, or to the side. Spoon the pan juices around the meat.

RISOTTO AL SALTO

≈≈≈

Fried Risotto

This Milanese recipe is supposed to have been invented as a way to
use up left-over risotto, but today it is regarded as a dish in its own right.
I recently visited 'Ristorante Peck' and found *Risotto al Salto* on the menu.
It is traditionally made with *Risotto alla Milanese* (see page 88),
but I prefer to use spinach or asparagus risotto.

SERVES 4

Risotto alla Milanese (see pages 88-9), or any left-over risotto
30g/1 oz (¼ stick) butter per person

Spread the risotto out on a large plate and run a fork or your fingers
through to separate the grains of rice.

If possible use a heavy omelet pan. Take a portion of risotto and flat-
ten it out to make a pizza shape smaller than the frying pan so that it can
slide about. Heat some butter in the pan and slide in the round of rice,
using the back of a wooden spoon to press it down. The rice will join
together. Cook slowly so that a crust is formed at the bottom. You can tell
when this has happened because the rice cake will slide across the pan
without sticking if you tilt the pan. Place a large plate over the frying pan
and turn upside down. Melt a little more butter and slide in the rice cake
to brown the other side.

MIROTON

≈≈

Beef and Rice Bake

I ate this dish in Piemonte when the first autumn mists came over the hillside vineyards. A glass of Nebbiolo completed the feast.

SERVES 6

75g/3 oz (¾ stick) butter
1 onion, 1 carrot and 1 celery stick, roughly chopped
500g/1 lb 2 oz piece of lean beef
1 bay leaf
4 peppercorns
salt
1 onion, finely chopped
500g/1 lb 2 oz (3 cups) Carnaroli rice (or Vialone nano or Arborio)
150ml/5 fl oz (⅔ cups) dry red wine
50g/2 oz (generous ½ cup) freshly grated Parmesan
2 eggs, beaten

Preheat the oven to 175°C/350°F.

Heat a little of the butter in a pan and gently cook the roughly chopped vegetables. Put in the meat and brown on all sides before adding 1.5 litres/2¾ pints (6 cups) boiling water, the bay leaf, peppercorns and salt. Cook until the meat is tender then remove with a slotted spoon, cut into slices and set to one side. Sieve the stock and spoon 4 tablespoons over the beef, reserving the rest.

Heat 30g/1 oz (¼ stick) of the butter in a large pan and gently cook the finely chopped onion until soft. Stir in the rice and after 5 minutes add the red wine and simmer until it has evaporated. Stir in the reserved beef stock a little at a time. After 10 minutes take the rice off the heat and stir in the Parmesan, eggs and remaining butter.

Grease a mold or soufflé dish and line with two thirds of the rice pushed against the bottom and sides. Spoon the beef and its juices into the middle and cover with the remaining rice smoothed over the top. Bake for 35 minutes then allow to stand for another 15 minutes before turning out on to a serving dish.

Riso in Cavroman

Lamb Risotto with Herbs and Spices

This spicy lamb risotto shows a Levantine influence, and
reminds us that Venice used to be Europe's gateway to Asia,
and the hub of the valuable spice trade.

Serves 4

2 tablespoons extra virgin olive oil
50g/2 oz (½ stick) butter
1 onion, finely chopped
2 cloves garlic, finely chopped
2 teaspoons chopped fresh rosemary
1 sage leaf, chopped
350g/12 oz lamb chops, with fat removed
100ml/3½ fl oz (½ cup) dry white wine
350g/12 oz fresh or canned Italian plum tomatoes, quartered and deseeded
2 cloves, 2cm cinnamon stick, ¼ teaspoon nutmeg, 1 bay leaf
salt and black pepper
1 litre/1¾ pints (4 cups) light meat stock
350g/12 oz (2 cups) Vialone nano rice (or Carnaroli or Arborio)
50g/2 oz (generous ½ cup) freshly grated Parmesan

Heat the oil and half the butter in a large pan and gently cook the onion,
garlic and fresh herbs. Add the meat, stir for a few minutes then pour on
the wine. When this has almost evaporated stir in the tomatoes, spices and
bay leaf. Season and add a little stock if necessary. Cook gently until the
meat is tender and comes easily away from the bone. Remove the bones
and tear the meat into small pieces. Return the meat to the pan and add
the remaining butter.

Stir in the rice and let it absorb some of the pan juices before adding
the boiling stock, a ladle at a time, waiting for the liquid to be absorbed
before adding more. When the rice is cooked, remove the whole spices
and stir in the cheese.

ARANCINE

'Little Oranges' or Fried Rice Balls

Arancine are sold all over Sicily from street stalls, *pizzerie* and snack bars. Sometimes they are as large as real oranges in order to allay hunger pangs, but when they are made as part of an *antipasti*, they are usually 4cm to 5cm (1½ to 2 in) in diameter. It is believed that the Arabs introduced this speciality to Sicily and similar recipes can be found in Arabic cuisine.

SERVES 4

2 tablespoons extra virgin olive oil
1 small onion, finely chopped
1 celery stick, finely chopped
200g/7 oz lean veal, chopped or minced
150g/5½ oz shelled peas
100ml/3½ fl oz (½ cup) fresh tomato sauce (see page 15)
1 litre/1¾ pints (4 cups) light meat stock
salt and black pepper
300g/10½ oz (1⅔ cups) Carnaroli rice (or Vialone nano or Arborio)
50g/2 oz (generous ½ cup) freshly grated caciocavallo cheese
or Parmesan
2 eggs, beaten
2 teaspoons saffron filaments, soaked in a little warm stock
pinch of grated nutmeg
30g/1 oz (¼ stick) butter, melted
plain (all-purpose) flour for dredging
dried breadcrumbs for coating
oil for deep-frying

Heat the olive oil in a large pan and gently cook the onion and celery until soft. Add the veal and when it has browned, stir in the peas, tomato sauce and some of the stock. Season, cover the pan and stew until the meat is tender and the liquid has almost evaporated. Bring half the stock to a boil and pour in the rice. Cook for 15 minutes, stirring occasionally and adding more stock if required until the rice is *al dente*. Drain, if necessary, and stir in the cheese, half the beaten egg, the strained saffron, the nutmeg, pepper and melted butter. Spread the mixture out on a large plate to cool.

To make the *arancine*, take a large spoonful of the rice, roll in your hand to form a ball then make a hollow in the center. Place a small spoonful of the meat mixture in the hole then cover with rice and close up the ball. Make all the balls in this way.

When ready to deep-fry, dredge each ball with flour, then dip in the remaining egg and roll in the breadcrumbs. Do not start to fry (see pages 4-5) until all the rice balls are ready. When cooked they should be golden brown to resemble oranges.

Risotto di Pasqua

Easter Lamb Risotto

Easter in Italy is always celebrated with young lamb on the
table in some form or another. In Puglia quince jelly lambs are
ordered in various sizes from the local convents famous for their sweets,
while in Sicily flocks of lambs are made from colored marzipan.
In Rome and the Abruzzo, the Italians are more prosaic and roast
or grill lamb with fresh rosemary and garlic, while in the
Veneto risotto is the order of the day.

Serves 4

50g/2 oz (½ stick) butter
1 clove garlic, minced
1 onion, 1 carrot and 1 celery stick, finely chopped
3 teaspoons finely chopped fresh rosemary
350g/12 oz lean lamb, cubed
salt and black pepper
100ml/3½ fl oz dry white wine
1.5 litres/2¾ pints (6 cups) light meat stock
350g/12 oz (2 cups) Vialone nano rice (or Carnaroli or Arborio)
zest of a large lemon
30g/1 oz (⅓ cup) freshly grated pecorino (optional)

Heat half the butter in a large pan and gently cook the vegetables until
soft. Add the rosemary and stir in the lamb. Season and pour over the
wine, stirring until it has evaporated. Add 300ml/10 fl oz (1¼ cups) of the
stock, bring to to a boil, cover and cook gently for 20 minutes. Stir in the
rice and add the rest of the stock a little at a time, waiting for the liquid
to be absorbed before stirring in more. Continue to cook, stirring, until all
the stock is absorbed by the rice. When the risotto is ready stir in the
lemon zest and remaining butter. Pecorino can be served at table if
required.

CHEESE

CHEESE

Italian cheeses are very exciting and each region has a cheese for every occasion. In the south of Italy there tends to be more sheep and goats' cheese because, traditionally, there were no herds of dairy cattle. *Parmigiano Reggiano* was, until fairly recently, an incredible luxury for the South. Even today it is often preferable to use local, hard grating cheeses rather than a ubiquitous Parmesan of uncertain quality.

Pecorino is the generic name given to all ewes' milk cheese. It can be fresh and soft – sold after the first salting, *primo sale* – or matured for eating and grating. Pecorino Romano comes from Rome while the other well-known and more pungent variety comes from Sardinia.

Mozzarella comes from Campania, but only the area near Battipaglia and Paestum have the traditional buffalos' milk variety. On the Amalfi Coast the mozzarella is made from cows' milk.

In the north of Italy we find Parmesan, fontina, Gorgonzola and a host of other great cheeses. Many of these are almost unknown outside their own region, and many never get exported.

When making these rice dishes always use good-quality cheese. Remember, rice is a neutral substance and the cheese enhances the flavor of the finished dish. Inferior cheese means, inevitably, an inferior taste. It is better to use good, local cheese, not packets of poor-quality grated Parmesan which has probably never seen Italy!

RISOTTO AI QUATTRO FORMAGGI

Risotto with Four Cheeses

If you prefer a milder taste, the Gorgonzola can be omitted
and replaced with another cheese.

SERVES 4

50g/2 oz (½ stick) butter
1 small onion, finely chopped
350g/12 oz (2 cups) Carnaroli rice (or Vialone nano or Arborio)
1.2 litres/2 pints (5 cups) light meat or vegetable stock
50g/2 oz taleggio cheese, diced
50g/2 oz fontina cheese, diced
50g/2 oz (generous ½ cup) freshly grated Parmesan
50g/2 oz Gorgonzola, diced
black pepper

Heat half the butter in a large pan and gently cook the onion until soft.
Stir in the rice and after 5 minutes start adding the boiling stock a ladle
at a time, waiting for the liquid to be absorbed before adding more. Keep
stirring and after 15 to 20 minutes, when the rice is cooked and the stock
is absorbed, stir in the cheeses and remaining butter. Add black pepper
and serve at once while the cheese is still creamy.

RISOTTO CON FONDUTA

≈

Risotto with Cheese Fonduta

Fonduta is a creamy cheese sauce which makes any dish very special.
If white or black truffles are grated over the top it becomes a fabulous
stravaganza. Sliced fried mushrooms can also be used.

SERVES 4

Fonduta
400g/14 oz fontina cheese from Val d'Aosta
200ml/7 fl oz (1 cup) milk
50g/2 oz (½ stick) butter
4 egg yolks

75g/3 oz (¾ stick) butter
1 onion, finely chopped
350g/12 oz (2 cups) Carnaroli rice (or Vialone nano or Arborio)
1 litre/1¾ pints (4 cups) light meat or vegetable stock
black pepper

To make the *Fonduta*, dice the cheese into very small pieces, cover with
the milk and leave for between 2 to 6 hours. Heat half the butter in a
double saucepan and put in the drained cheese, stirring all the time with
a wooden spoon. The mixture must not boil. Turn up the heat and
vigorously stir in the yolks, one at a time. Stir in the remaining butter and
keep warm until ready to use.

To make the risotto, heat half the butter in a large pan and gently
cook the onion until soft. Add the rice and stir for 5 minutes then start to
pour the stock in gradually, a ladle at a time, until after 15 to 20 minutes
it is all absorbed and the rice is cooked.

Serve the risotto covered in the *Fonduta* like a cream sauce. Grind on
some fresh black pepper if no truffles or mushrooms are to hand.

SUPPLÌ

≈

Fried Rice Croquettes Stuffed with Mozzarella

These crunchy rice croquettes are a Roman speciality usually sold
and eaten as street food to provide a delicious hot snack. They are
so popular they are often found in *pizzerie* too. The mozzarella
cheese in the middle pulls out as they are eaten, looking rather like
telephone cables (*supplì*) which gives them their Italian name.

MAKES 18 CROQUETTES

400g/14 oz (2⅓ cups) Carnaroli rice
(or Arborio or Vialone nano)
salt
100g/4 oz (1 stick) butter
150g/5½ oz (scant 2 cups) freshly grated Parmesan
2 eggs, beaten
black pepper
100g/4 oz ham or salami
300g/10½ oz mozzarella cheese
2 eggs, beaten, flour and breadcrumbs to coat the croquettes
oil for deep-frying

Cook the rice in 1.5 litres/2¾ pints (6 cups) boiling, salted water for 12 to
15 minutes. Drain and while it is still hot, stir in the butter, Parmesan,
beaten eggs and black pepper. Allow to cool. Dice the ham or salami and
mozzarella to form the filling. When the rice is cool divide the mixture
into 18 balls and with your thumb make a hole in each one. Fill the holes
with the ham and cheese cubes, then form the filled balls into smooth,
slightly elongated croquettes. Dust with flour, roll in egg then breadcrumbs and deep-fry (see page 4) until golden brown.

RISOTTO CON GORGONZOLA

≋

Gorgonzola Risotto

This simple recipe from Lombardy pleases the lovers
of this pungent blue cheese.

SERVES 4

300g/10½ oz Gorgonzola, chopped
1 litre/1¾ pints (4 cups) light meat or vegetable stock
50g/2 oz (½ stick) butter
1 small onion, finely chopped
300g/10½ oz (1⅔ cups) Carnaroli rice (or Vialone nano or Arborio)
salt and black pepper
8 walnut halves, chopped

Put the chopped Gorgonzola in a pan with a little of the hot stock and stir
to make a thick cream. Heat half the butter in a separate large pan and
cook the onion gently until soft. Stir in the rice and after 5 minutes start
adding the remaining stock, which should be boiling, a little at a time.
After 15 to 20 minutes the rice should be cooked. Remove from the heat,
season, stir in the remaining butter and serve with the melted Gorgonzola
poured over the top. Sprinkle each serving with chopped walnuts.

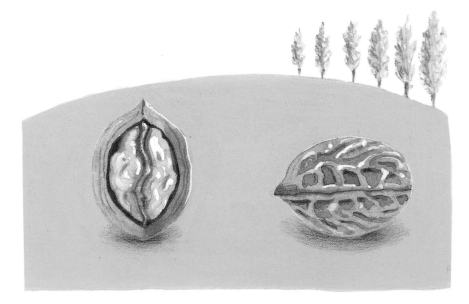

RISO AI FORMAGGI

Baked Rice with Cheese

Although it is not orthodox, when I make this Piemonte rice dish
I like to add some finely sliced onion cooked until soft in olive oil in place
of the ham. Different cheeses can be used if preferred.

SERVES 4

400g/14 oz (2⅓ cups) Carnaroli rice (or Vialone nano or Arborio)
100g/4 oz (1 stick) butter
50g/2 oz (generous ½ cup) freshly grated Parmesan
salt and black pepper
50g/2 oz fontina cheese from Val d'Aosta, sliced thinly
50g/2 oz provolone cheese, sliced thinly
50g/2 oz (generous ½ cup) shaved Parmesan
75g/3 oz lean cooked ham, sliced thinly

Preheat oven to 180°C/350°F and butter a large ovenproof dish.

Bring 1.5 litres/2¾ pints (6 cups) lightly salted water to a boil in a
large pan and cook the rice for 8 minutes. Drain and set aside.

Melt half the butter in another large pan and stir in the rice. Keep
stirring for 5 minutes then add three quarters of the grated Parmesan and
season. Smooth one third of the rice over the bottom of the ovenproof
dish and make a layer over the top with half the sliced cheeses, the shaved
Parmesan and ham. Make another layer of rice and cover with the
remaining cheese and ham slices. Spread the remaining rice over the top,
melt the remaining butter and sprinkle it on with the remaining grated
Parmesan. Sprinkle on a little freshly ground black pepper and bake for
15 minutes.

SFORMATINI DI RISO

Individual Baked Rice Molds with Béchamel Sauce

These little rice molds make a very
delicious starter or accompaniment
to a meal.

SERVES 4

30g/1 oz (¼ stick) butter
300g/10½ oz (2 cups) Carnaroli rice
(or Vialone nano or Arborio)

Béchamel Sauce
30g/1 oz (¼ stick) butter
30g/1 oz (scant ¼ cup) plain (all-purpose) flour
300ml/10 fl oz (1¼ cups) milk
pinch of grated nutmeg
salt and black pepper

50g/2 oz (generous ½ cup) freshly grated Parmesan
120g/4½ oz mozzarella, diced
black pepper
1 tablespoon dried breadcrumbs

Preheat the oven to 175°C/350°F and butter four 3 ½ oz molds.

Bring 750ml/1¼ pints lightly salted water to a boil in a large pan.
Pour in the rice, simmer for 10 minutes and drain.

Meanwhile, make the béchamel sauce. Melt the butter in a small
saucepan and stir in the flour. Cook for a few minutes stirring all the time.
Gradually stir in the milk over a low heat and continue stirring until the
sauce is thick and smooth. Add the nutmeg and seasoning.

Stir the béchamel sauce, Parmesan, mozzarella and a little black
pepper into the cooked rice. Dust the buttered molds with the breadcrumbs and spoon in the rice mixture, levelling the tops. Bake for 15 to
20 minutes until golden brown, remove from the oven and leave to stand
for another 5 minutes. Turn out and serve on individual plates, browned
side up.

Crostata di Riso
≈≈
Baked Rice with Mozzarella

The first time I ate this Neapolitan specialty I was sitting on
the shady terrace of a villa in Ischia, listening to the cicadas and lazily
contemplating a late afternoon swim. In the end I ate so much *Crostata di
Riso* that my hosts suggested I postpone the swim for fear of sinking!

SERVES 4

2 tablespoons extra virgin olive oil
1 large onion, finely chopped
1 litre/1¾ pints (4 cups) light stock or water
400g/14 oz (2⅓ cups) Carnaroli rice (or Vialone nano or Arborio)
500ml/18 fl oz (2 cups) fresh tomato sauce (see page 15)
1 tablespoon finely chopped fresh parsley
salt and black pepper
100g/4 oz (1¼ cups) freshly grated Parmesan
6 basil leaves, torn
300g/10½ oz mozzarella, sliced
30g/1 oz (¼ stick) butter

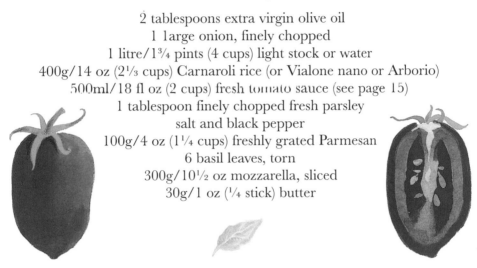

Preheat the oven to 175°C/350°F and lightly oil a large round
ovenproof dish.

Heat the remaining oil in a large pan and gently cook the onion until
soft. In another pan, bring the stock to a boil and pour in the rice. Simmer
for 10 minutes then drain and stir the rice into the onion
mixture. Cook for 5 minutes and mix in three quarters of the tomato
sauce with the parsley and seasoning. Stir in three quarters of the
Parmesan and the basil and spoon half the rice mixture into the
ovenproof dish, levelling the top. Cover with the mozzarella slices and
top with the remaining sauce. Make another layer with the remaining
rice and sprinkle over the remaining Parmesan. Dot with butter and bake
for 35 minutes. Remove from the oven and leave to stand for 10 minutes
before serving.

FRITTATA DI RISO

Rice Omelet

Any left-over risotto can be used for this recipe. However it is such
a tasty dish in its own right I often make the rice specially for the *frittata*.
In Campania in the south, rice and pasta *frittate* are made as part of a
delicious picnic so that no one has to go without their *primo* or first course.
It is equally delicious cold or hot.

SERVES 4

Left-over risotto, or 300g/10½ oz (1⅔ cups) Carnaroli rice
(or Vialone nano or Arborio)
50g/2 oz (generous ½ cup) freshly grated Parmesan
2 eggs, beaten
6 tablespoons fresh tomato sauce (see page 15)
2 teaspoons chopped fresh parsley
4 basil leaves
salt and black pepper
50g/2 oz (¼ stick) – 100g/4 oz (½ stick) butter for frying

You need a heavy bottomed frying pan. If it is large, make two *frittate*. If
it is smaller, make four.

If you have no left-over risotto, cook the rice in double the quantity
of boiling salted water for 10 minutes and drain. Stir all the other
ingredients except for the butter into the cooked rice or risotto.

For each *frittata* melt 15g/½ oz (⅛ stick) butter in the pan. Put in
enough rice mixture to make a flat, even pizza-like round. Cook on a very
low heat, turning the pan round slowly clockwise so that it cooks evenly.
When the bottom has turned crisp and golden, cover the pan with a large
plate, invert it to turn out the *frittata*, add more butter to the pan and cook
the other side in the same way. Don't get tempted to hurry the procedure.
The end result will be worth your patience.

STRAVAGANZA

STRAVAGANZA

≈≈

In Italy food excites as much passion as love – sometimes even more – and shopping becomes a sensuous adventure. Everyday vegetables are lovingly handled as they are held out to be admired and a humble head of celery is tenderly wrapped in paper before being tucked away in a shopping bag. Even a good steak is beautiful – *una bella bistecca* – and choosing or rejecting fish becomes an emotional quicksand.

When so much sentiment is invested in the daily meal, what do you do to make something really special? In this section I have grouped together a collection of recipes that use extravagant ingredients or a prodigious amount of effort to create excitement and pleasure for your family and friends. Enjoy them.

RISOTTO DELLE ROSE

≈

Rose Petal Risotto

This decadent risotto from
Lake Garda was served in the 1930s
to the poet Gabriele D'Annunzio at his romantic
dinners with the actress Eleonora Duse.

SERVES 4

4 pink rosebuds, just opening out
120g/4½ oz (1 stick) butter
350g/12 oz (2 cups) Vialone nano rice (or Carnaroli or Arborio)
pinch of grated nutmeg
150ml/5 fl oz (²⁄₃ cups) dry rosé or white wine
1 litre/1¾ pints (4 cups) light meat or vegetable stock
salt and black pepper
100ml/3½ fl oz (½ cup) double (heavy) cream
a few drops of pink coloring (optional)
1 teaspoon rose water (optional)
120g/4½ oz Emmenthal cheese shavings

Wash the roses and take off the petals. Reserve 8 perfect petals for
decoration and divide the rest into pale and deeper pink. Heat half the
butter in a large pan and stir in the rice, a pinch of grated nutmeg and
the pale petals and cook for 5 minutes.

Pour in the wine and continue cooking until it has almost evaporated.
Start stirring in the stock a ladle at a time, waiting for the liquid to be
absorbed before adding more. After 10 minutes stir in the darker petals
and continue to cook for 5 to 10 minutes until the rice is *al dente*. Take off
the heat, adjust the seasoning and add the remaining butter and cream.
At this point a few drops of pink coloring and the rose water can be
added.

Serve covered with shavings of cheese and the reserved petals
arranged on top.

RISOTTO ALLO SPUMANTE

Champagne Risotto

A rich, opulent risotto from Piemonte, home of the great
red wines, but also producer of some good dry sparkling wines.
A risotto for a very special occasion.

SERVES 4

1 bottle champagne or good dry sparkling wine
350g/12 oz (2 cups) Carnaroli rice
(or Vialone nano or Arborio)
50g/2 oz (½ stick) butter
2 celery sticks, finely chopped
1 small onion, finely chopped
1 small leek, cut into thin rings
1 bay leaf
1 litre/1¾ pints (4 cups) light meat or vegetable stock
50g/2 oz (generous ½ cup) freshly grated Parmesan
250ml/9 fl oz (generous 1 cup) double (heavy) cream
salt and white pepper

Keep 4 tablespoons of champagne to one side and soak the rice in the rest
of it for 30 minutes. Heat half the butter in a large pan and gently stew
the vegetables until soft. Add the bay leaf. In a separate pan bring the
stock to a boil and allow to simmer. Using a perforated spoon, lift the rice
out of the champagne and stir into the vegetables. The rice should not be
completely drained. Cook the rice, stirring continuously and add any
remaining champagne a ladle at a time. When the champagne has all
been absorbed by the rice, start to use the stock. After 15 to 20 minutes,
the rice will be cooked but still *al dente*. Remove from the heat and stir in
the reserved champagne, the remaining butter, the Parmesan and the
cream. Season with salt and freshly ground white pepper, stir and serve.

RISOTTO AL BALSAMICO

Risotto with Traditional Balsamic Vinegar

My favorite restaurant in Bologna is 'Silverio'. Silverio Cineri
is a genial, relaxed host and an imaginative chef. He invents and
improvises as he goes along. He is also a great enthusiast and
he has intriguing collections of antique pasta implements, prints
and traditional balsamic vinegars.
Traditional balsamic vinegar is made in Modena, takes many years
to perfect and starts with the cooked *must* of the Trebbiano grape. The
vinegar is stored in a series of casks made of oak, chestnut, cherry, ash and
mulberry. When small quantities are eventually bottled they have a sweet,
smooth, rounded taste which bears no resemblance to the acid-tasting
vinegars found on supermarket shelves. The real thing will be
expensive and labelled 'traditional' not just 'Modena'.

SERVES 4

50g/2 oz (½ stick) butter
1 small onion, finely chopped
200g/7 oz (scant 1¼ cups) Carnaroli rice (or Vialone nano or Arborio)
1 litre/1¾ pints (4 cups) light meat or vegetable stock
50g/2 oz (generous ½ cup) freshly grated Parmesan
salt
4 teaspoons traditional balsamic vinegar from Modena
30g/1 oz (⅓ cup) Parmesan shavings

Melt half the butter in a pan and gently cook the onion until soft. Add the
rice and stir around the pan for about 5 minutes. Start adding the boiling
stock ladle by ladle until the rice is cooked. It will take about 20 minutes.
Add a little boiling water if you run out of stock. Turn off the heat and
beat in the remaining butter and grated Parmesan and season. Serve at
once, drizzling 1 teaspoon balsamic vinegar in the center of each serving,
partially covered by shavings of Parmesan.

RISOTTO AL BAROLO

≈≈

Risotto in Barolo Red Wine

This is a luxurious recipe from Piemonte, home of the great
red wines. It is important to use a really good wine, at least three
years old, not the dregs of an already opened bottle!
The last time I visited 'La Contea' restaurant in Neive, my colleague
bought a 40-year-old Barolo as a birthday present for her husband to
console him for reaching the same milestone. I was tempted to search
for a similar bottle for a very special risotto, but I was deterred by the
realization that I would need several bottles to drink with the
risotto and would end up with a *Babette's Feast* situation!

SERVES 4

30g/1 oz (¼ stick) butter
1 small onion, finely chopped
350g/12 oz (2 cups) Carnaroli rice (or Vialone nano or Arborio)
500ml/18 fl oz (2 cups) Barolo red wine
500ml/18 fl oz (2 cups) rich meat or vegetable stock
salt and black pepper
50g/2 oz (generous ½ cup) freshly grated Parmesan

Melt half the butter in a large pan and gently cook the onion until soft.
Add the rice and stir with the onion for about 5 minutes. Start to stir in
the wine a ladle at a time, and when that is finished continue with the
boiling stock. Keep stirring until the rice is cooked *al dente*, after 15 to 20
minutes. Take off the heat, check the seasoning, stir in the remaining
butter and Parmesan and serve at once.

Riso col Limone

Lemon Risotto

Before industrial development, *la Conca d'Oro*
in Sicily used to be a sea of orange and lemon
trees. Sadly this has disappeared but Sicilian citrus
fruit still give a very special flavor to many dishes.
In Sicily oranges are considered better with fish than lemons, which are
used mainly for sweet dishes. However, this risotto is an exception.
Cheese can be served separately or stirred in at the end of cooking,
or for a light and delicate flavor omit the cheese.

Serves 4

30g/1 oz (¼ stick) butter
1 small onion, finely chopped
400g/14 oz (2⅓ cups) Carnaroli rice (or Vialone nano or Arborio)
100ml/3½ fl oz (½ cup) dry white wine
juice and zest of 1 juicy lemon
1 litre/1¾ pints (4 cups) light meat or vegetable stock
1 tablespoon finely chopped fresh parsley
salt and black pepper
50g/2 oz (generous ½ cup) freshly grated caciocavallo cheese
or Parmesan (optional)

Melt the butter in a large pan and gently cook the onion until soft. Stir in
the rice and after 5 minutes add the wine and half the lemon zest. Stir in
the boiling stock a ladle at a time and after 15 to 20 minutes, when the
rice is cooked *al dente*, turn off the heat and stir in the parsley, lemon juice,
remaining lemon zest, salt and pepper. If using cheese, it can either be
stirred in or handed round separately.

Sartù in Sfoglia di Melanzane

≈≈≈

Individual Sartù Lined with Eggplant

This elegant *Sartù* was created by Livia and Alfonso Iaccarino in their three-star Michelin restaurant, 'Don Alfonso', on the Amalfi coast at Sant'Agata sui due Golfi. This is one of my favorite restaurants, serving creative innovations and traditional Neapolitan dishes with a lighter interpretation. They use superb local ingredients, many of them grown organically on Alfonso's farm facing Capri.

SERVES 4

2 eggplants, finely sliced
coarse salt for purging
oil for frying

Tomato Sauce
1 tablespoon extra virgin olive oil
1 small onion, chopped
50g/2 oz carrot, chopped
50g/2 oz celery, chopped
500g/1 lb 2 oz canned Italian plum tomatoes
1 bay leaf
80g/3 oz lean meat, finely chopped
salt and black pepper

Meatballs
150g/5½ oz ground meat
1 slice stale bread, crusts removed,
soaked in milk
1 egg yolk
salt and black pepper
pinch of grated nutmeg
plain (all-purpose) flour for dredging
1 tablespoon extra virgin olive oil

2 chicken livers, chopped (optional)
2 tablespoons brandy

2 tablespoons extra virgin olive oil
300g/10½ oz (1⅔ cups) Carnaroli rice (or Vialone nano or Arborio)
150g/5½ oz shelled peas
1 onion, finely chopped
50ml/2 fl oz (¼ cup) dry white wine
1 litre/1 ¾ pints (4 cups) light meat stock
1 tablespoon freshly grated Parmesan
2 egg yolks
150g/5½ oz mozzarella, diced

1 tablespoon dried breadcrumbs
basil leaves for decoration (optional)

Preheat the oven to 180°C/350°F and grease four 3 ½ oz molds.

Purge the eggplant slices of their bitter juices (see page 13). Rinse well and pat dry. Fry until golden brown and leave to drain on paper towels.

Meanwhile, make the tomato sauce by heating the oil in a pan and gently cooking the onion, carrot and celery until soft. Blend or process the mixture to make a smooth paste. Return to the pan and add the tomatoes, bay leaf and meat. Season and leave to cook for 30 minutes. Pass through a mouli or sieve.

Make the meatballs by blending the minced meat, soaked bread, egg yolk, seasoning and nutmeg in a food processor. Roll into tiny balls, dredge in the flour and fry in the olive oil until golden brown. Drain on paper towels. If using chicken livers in the risotto, stir-fry them in the meatball oil for 5 minutes, season and pour over the brandy.

To make the risotto, heat the oil in a large pan and gently stir the rice around in it for 5 minutes. Add the peas and onion. Pour on the wine and a little of the stock and keep stirring for 10 minutes. When the rice is half cooked spread the mixture out on a large plate to cool. Place in a bowl and stir in the Parmesan and egg yolks. Add the mozzarella, meatballs and chicken livers if using.

Line the molds with the breadcrumbs and then the slices of eggplant. Pack in the rice mixture and bake for 15 minutes. Remove the molds from the oven and leave to stand for 5 minutes. Spoon some tomato sauce on each plate then turn out the *Sartù* on top. Decorate with basil leaves if available and serve.

RISOTTO CON FIORI DI ZUCCHINI

Risotto with Zucchini Flowers

In some countries zucchini flowers are so expensive,
when you can find them, that this dish can be classified as a *stravaganza*.
However, in Rome you can buy eight blossoms for less than two dollars
and the same amount with get you two pounds of them in southern Italy!
There the plants are grown specifically for their flowers, so there is no
minute vegetable attached, although you can also buy zucchinis
with flowers, too. If the flowers do have zucchinis
attached, slice some of them very finely and
add them to the risotto after the onion
and before the rice.

SERVES 4

8 zucchini flowers
80g/3 oz (¾ stick) butter
1 onion, finely chopped
350g/12 oz (2 cups) Vialone nano rice (or Carnaroli or Arborio)
1 litre/1¾ pints (4 cups) light meat or vegetable stock
salt and black pepper
50g/2 oz (generous ½ cup) freshly grated Parmesan
4 basil leaves, roughly torn

Remove the stalk, stamens and pistils from the flowers and cut off the
zucchinis if necessary, slicing them thinly and discarding the thick join.
Dip the flowers gently in a bowl of water to float out any dust or insects
then pat dry and cut into ribbons.

Heat half the butter in a large pan and gently cook the onion until
soft. If you have some zucchinis to use add them now. Add the rice and
stir for 5 minutes before starting to add the stock a ladle at a time, waiting
for the liquid to be absorbed before stirring in more. After 15 minutes,
when the rice is almost cooked, add the flowers and stir well. Remove
from the heat, adjust the seasoning and stir in the Parmesan, basil and the
rest of the butter. Serve with freshly ground black pepper.

117

RISO IN PADELLA

Rice in the Frying Pan

When I first discovered this Sicilian recipe, I was amazed to recognize *paella*. It is thought that the Arabs introduced the first versions of this dish to western Europe, but nobody knows whether Spain or Sicily was the first to adopt and adapt it. It is interesting to see that in both cases the dish is named after the pot in which it is cooked and served – the *padella* is a shallow frying pan.

SERVES 6

1kg/2 lb 4 oz mussels in their shells
150ml/5 fl oz (⅔ cup) dry white wine
6 tablespoons extra virgin olive oil
1 chicken breast fillet, cut into pieces
1 chicken leg, boned and cut into pieces
1 hot Italian sausage, sliced
300g/10½ oz squid, cleaned and cut into rings
300g/10½ oz prawns (shrimps), shelled and de-veined
1 onion, finely chopped
2 cloves garlic, finely chopped
2 red (bell or sweet) peppers
200g/7 oz shelled peas
200g/7 oz canned Italian plum tomatoes, chopped
2 tablespoons finely chopped fresh parsley
salt and black pepper
2 teaspoons saffron filaments
300g/10½ oz (1⅔ cups) Carnaroli rice (or Vialone nano or Arborio)

Scrape the mussels under running water, removing the 'beard' and discarding any open or broken shells. Put them in a pan with half the wine and a little water. Cover and bring quickly to a boil so that the shells open. Discard any that fail to open. Strain, put to one side and keep the liquid.

Heat 4 tablespoons oil in another pan and cook the chicken and sausage for 10 minutes. Remove with a slotted spoon and keep to one side. In the same oil cook the squid and prawns for 5 minutes before removing with a slotted spoon and setting aside. Heat 2 more tablespoons of oil in the same pan and cook the onion and garlic for a few minutes.

Cut the peppers into strips, removing the seeds and fibers and stir them into the pan with the peas and tomatoes. Add the parsley and season. Cook for 10 minutes and return the chicken, sausage and two thirds of the shellfish to the pan.

Soak the saffron in a little warm stock then strain and pour the liquid into the pan, together with the reserved mussel liquid. Bring to a boil then stir in the rice. Start to add the stock a little at a time, stirring frequently.

After 15 minutes check to see if a wooden spoon can stand up by itself in the mixture. If not, you need to continue cooking a little longer to absorb more of the stock. When it is ready, stir a final time to distribute all the ingredients equally and spoon the remaining shellfish over the top.

TUMMÀLA

Christmas Sicilian Baked Rice Timballo

This great, opulent dish is served for important celebrations. Although it looks complicated, the chicken and meatballs can be prepared the day before and the *timballo* assembled several hours in advance. It is another dish that shows the Arabic influence on Sicilian cuisine. The name comes from Mohammed ibn ath-Thumma who was the Emir of Catania during the days of Arab rule.

SERVES 8

Chicken and Stock
1.5kg/3 lb 5 oz chicken, cleaned
1 onion, 1 carrot and 1 celery stick, roughly chopped
2 tablespoons fresh tomato sauce (see page 15)
1 bay leaf and 2 cloves
6 peppercorns
salt

Meatballs
1 slice coarse stale bread, crusts removed, soaked in milk
250g/9 oz lean veal or beef
30g/1 oz ($\frac{1}{3}$ cup) freshly grated pecorino
1 egg, beaten
1 tablespoon chopped fresh parsley
pinch of grated nutmeg
salt and black pepper
2 tablespoons extra virgin olive oil

Timballo
200g/7 oz lean Italian fresh sausage
400g/14 oz ($2\frac{1}{3}$ cups) Carnaroli rice (or Arborio or Vialone nano)
50g/2 oz (generous $\frac{1}{2}$ cup) freshly grated caciocavallo cheese or pecorino
100g/4 oz ($1\frac{1}{4}$ cups) freshly grated pecorino
250ml/9 fl oz (generous 1 cup) fresh tomato sauce (see page 15)
250g/9 oz tuma cheese or mozzarella, sliced
3 eggs, beaten
black pepper

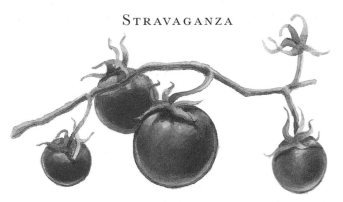

Grease an ovenproof dish of about 30cm/12 in diameter and 15cm/6 in depth.

To cook the chicken and make the stock, cover the bird and other stock ingredients with 2 litres/3½ pints (8 cups) cold water in a large pan and bring to a boil. Cover and simmer for 45 minutes. Discard the skin and bones, cut the meat into small pieces and set aside. Pour the stock through a strainer and reserve.

While making the meatballs, preheat the oven to 180°C/350°F.

Squeeze the milk from the bread and put all the meatball ingredients except the olive oil in a food processor. Process to make a smooth paste. Roll into small balls about the size of a walnut. Heat the oil and fry half the meatballs until golden brown. The remaining meatballs should be simmered gently for 15 minutes in some of the chicken stock.

To make the *timballo*, prick the sausage in a pan of boiling water so that the fat runs out and simmer for 10 minutes. When cooked cut into slices and set aside. Boil the rice in 1 litre/1¾ pints (4 cups) chicken stock in another pan for 10 minutes. Cover, remove from the heat and let it rest for 10 minutes. At the end of this time the stock should all be absorbed. Stir in the caciocavallo and half the pecorino and set aside. Heat the tomato sauce and stir in the sausage and fried meatballs.

To bake, arrange one third of the rice mixture over the bottom of the oven dish. Cover with two thirds of the chicken meat and soft meatballs and arrange the slices of tuma or mozzarella cheese on top. Then cover with half the remaining rice and layer on the tomato, sausage and fried meatball mixture. Stir the remaining chicken into the remaining rice and spoon over the top. Beat the remaining pecorino into the eggs and pour over the dish. Grind on black pepper.

Bake for 45 minutes until the crust is golden brown. Cover the dish if it starts to get too brown.

SARTÙ

≈≈

Neapolitan Baked Rice

This is one of the traditional, elaborate masterpieces, brought to
Naples by the French chefs. To serve, the rice is turned out and the
remaining sauce is poured over the top, giving the dish the French name
Surtout which evolved into *Sartù*. In the past it was heavy and complicated,
stuffed with a variety of meat, offal and truffles. The French chefs insisted
on being called '*monsieur*' and, since the Neapolitans could not get
their tongue round the French title, they called them '*monzù*'. Today,
the *monzù* have given their name to a complicated, baroque style of
cooking found in the Neapolitan and Sicilian culinary tradition.
This *Sartù* is a lighter, modern version, which can also be made
in individual molds as an elegant starter (see page 114).

SERVES 6

dried breadcrumbs
2 quantities of tomato sauce (see page 15)
500g/1 lb 2 oz (3 cups) Carnaroli rice (or Arborio or Vialone nano)
100g/4 oz (1¼ cups) freshly grated Parmesan
2 eggs, beaten
1 tablespoon chopped fresh parsley
salt and black pepper

Filling
¼ quantity of meatballs (see page 120)
4 tablespoons olive oil
150g/5½ oz shelled peas
30g/1 oz (¼ stick) butter, melted
salt and black pepper
150g/5½ oz mozzarella, sliced
150g/5½ oz cooked ham, cut in batons
2 hard-boiled eggs, each cut into 8 segments

Preheat the oven to 180°C/350°F and lightly oil a mold about 12cm/4½
in depth and 15cm/6 in diameter, or a large brioche tin, and line with
breadcrumbs.

Make the tomato sauce, and put half into a heavy saucepan with
enough water to make 1 litre/1¾ pints (4 cups). Bring to a boil and pour

in the rice. Cover and cook slowly for 15 minutes, without stirring or removing the lid. Turn the rice into a large bowl, and when it has cooled slightly stir in the Parmesan, beaten eggs, parsley and seasoning.

Make the meatballs the size of large cherries and fry until golden brown in the olive oil. Coat them with some of the remaining tomato sauce and keep to one side. Cook the peas until tender in lightly salted boiling water, drain and dress with the melted butter and a little black pepper.

Arrange two thirds of the rice in the mold, making a layer about 1 inch deep at the bottom and pushing the rest against the sides of the dish with a wooden spoon. Fill the middle with layers of mozzarella, ham, peas, hard-boiled eggs and the meatballs. Cover with the remaining rice and sprinkle more breadcrumbs over the top.

Bake for about 45 minutes. The top should be golden brown, but cover with foil if it turns brown too quickly. Remove from the oven and leave to stand for 15 minutes before turning out on a warm serving plate. Serve with the remaining tomato sauce passed round in a sauce boat.

BOMBA DI RISO

Rice Bomb

Traditionally this rich, elaborate rice 'bomb' is prepared in
Piacenza, in the Po Valley, for the *Festa della Madonna* on 15 August.
It is usually made with pigeon but I find it easier to substitute duck or
guinea fowl. The technique can be adapted for any meat. Traditionally
it is cooked in a deep, round mold but a pudding basin will also work.
In Parma it can be ordered in advance at the 'Ristorante Cocchi'.

SERVES 6

125g/4½ oz (1⅛ sticks) butter
1 onion, finely sliced
1 small pigeon, or duck, guinea fowl or chicken on the bone, cut into pieces
3 sage leaves
3 juniper berries, crushed
salt and black pepper
100ml/4 fl oz (½ cup) dry white wine
1 tablespoon fresh tomato sauce (see page 15)
500g/1 lb 2 oz (3 cups) Carnaroli rice (or Vialone nano or Arborio)
50g/2 oz (generous ½ cup) freshly grated Parmesan
2 eggs, beaten
2 tablespoons fresh soft breadcrumbs

Preheat the oven to 170°C/325°F.

Melt 30g/1 oz (¼ stick) of the butter in a large pan, let the onion
soften and gently brown the whole pigeon with the sage, juniper, salt, and
pepper. Stir in the wine and cook for a few minutes, then add the
tomato sauce and 200ml/7 fl oz (1 cup) of boiling water. Cover and cook
until the meat is tender, adding a little more liquid if it gets too dry. Using
a slotted spoon, lift out the pigeon and remove the meat from the bones.
Chop the meat, set to one side and sieve the sauce.

Boil the rice in a large pan of lightly salted water, or stock made from
the pigeon carcass, for 8 minutes, then drain and stir in half the sieved
sauce, 50g/2 oz (½ stick) butter, the Parmesan and the beaten eggs.

Butter the mold and line with two thirds of the breadcrumbs. This
will form a golden crust when the 'bomb' is turned out. Spoon in two
thirds of the rice, pressing against the bottom and sides of the mold to

leave a hole in the middle. Fill this with the pigeon meat and remaining sauce and cover with the rest of the rice.

Melt the remaining butter and scatter on top with the rest of the breadcrumbs. Bake until a golden crust forms. Remove and let it stand for another 10 minutes before turning out on to a serving dish.

CRESPELLE DI RISO

Sweet Rice Fritters

In Sicily the convents are famous for their desserts, and in the past many nuns from wealthy families relieved the monotony of cloistered life by concocting elaborate cakes. It is unusual to find monks inventing similar delights but this recipe comes from the Benedictine monastery in Catania. The fritters are traditionally eaten on St Joseph's day, March 19, which is also Father's Day in Italy.

SERVES 4

250g/9 oz (scant 1½ cups) Arborio rice (or Carnaroli or Vialone nano)
250ml/9 fl oz (generous 1 cup) milk
150g/5 oz fresh ricotta cheese
100g/4 oz (¾ cup) plain (all-purpose) flour
zest of 1 lemon and 1 orange
12g/¼ oz fresh yeast
oil for deep-frying
1 tablespoon icing sugar
1 teaspoon cinnamon
6 tablespoons honey, preferably orange or lemon flower

Bring the rice to a boil in a pan with the milk and equal quantity of water. Cook gently, stirring, until the liquid is absorbed and the rice is soft. This will take about 20 minutes. Spread out on a plate, cover and leave for several hours, preferably overnight. Transfer to a large bowl and stir in the ricotta, flour, citrus zest and the yeast dissolved in a little warm water. Cover and leave for 1 hour. When ready to serve shape the mixture into pieces about 15cm/6 in long, 2cm/¾ in wide and 2cm/¾ in high. Deep-fry the fritters in hot oil in batches (see page 4). Dust with sifted icing sugar and cinnamon. Serve at once with the honey spooned on top.

Risotto al Tartufo Bianco

Risotto with White Truffles

Piemonte is a mecca for the *buongustaio* during the white truffle season, which starts in October and finishes at the end of December. It is considered a great achievement to find a truffle for New Year's Eve. It could be considered an even greater achievement to be able to afford it, since in 1999 white truffles cost $300 for 100g/4 oz!

Serves 4

100g/4 oz (1 stick) butter
1 small shallot, finely chopped
300g/10½ oz (1⅔ cups) Carnaroli rice (or Vialone nano or Arborio)
1 litre/1¾ pints (4 cups) light meat or vegetable stock
100g/4 oz (1¼ cups) freshly grated Parmesan
40g/1½ oz white truffle, brushed and cleaned

Heat half the butter in a large pan and cook the shallot gently until soft. Stir in the rice and after 5 minutes start adding the boiling stock a little at a time, waiting for the liquid to be absorbed before adding more. Keep stirring and after 15 to 20 minutes, the rice should be cooked *al dente*. Take off the heat, beat in the remaining butter and Parmesan and serve. Shave the truffle over the individual plates so that everyone can feast on its delicious aroma before they begin to eat.

RISOTTO ALLA ROBIOLA E TARTUFO NERO

≈≈

Risotto with Robiola Cheese and Black Truffles

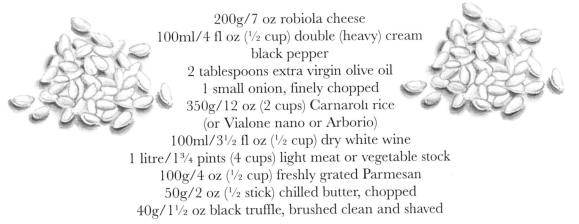

Robiola is a soft creamy cheese found in good cheese shops and
some Italian grocers. It can be replaced by any other soft cheese if
not available. Angelo Angiuli prepares this dish during the black truffle
season – December to the end of March – at his Piemonte restaurant
in the charming little medieval town of Candelo.
It is not worth using summer truffles as they have little flavor.
What the cream, cheese and butter might do to your arteries
is justified by the exquisite taste of this risotto!

SERVES 4

200g/7 oz robiola cheese
100ml/4 fl oz (½ cup) double (heavy) cream
black pepper
2 tablespoons extra virgin olive oil
1 small onion, finely chopped
350g/12 oz (2 cups) Carnaroli rice
(or Vialone nano or Arborio)
100ml/3½ fl oz (½ cup) dry white wine
1 litre/1¾ pints (4 cups) light meat or vegetable stock
100g/4 oz (½ cup) freshly grated Parmesan
50g/2 oz (½ stick) chilled butter, chopped
40g/1½ oz black truffle, brushed clean and shaved

Mix together the robiola and cream over a gentle heat to make a thick,
smooth sauce. Season with black pepper. Heat the oil in a large pan and
gently cook the onion until soft. Stir in the rice and after 5 minutes add
the wine. When this has evaporated start to add the stock a little at a time,
waiting for the liquid to be absorbed before stirring in more. The rice will
take about 20 minutes to cook.

Remove from the heat and stir in the Parmesan and butter. Serve on
to individual plates. Make a hole in the middle of each serving of rice and
fill with the robiola sauce. Arrange the truffle shavings over the top.

CORONA DI PRIMAVERA

≈≈≈

Crown of Rice with Spring Vegetables

The style of presentation of this dish can be used for many other recipes in this book. The vegetables can be varied according to the season.

SERVES 4

Vegetable Center
2 zucchinis, diced
200g/7 oz shelled fava beans
200g/7 oz shelled peas
200g/7 oz fine asparagus tips
sprig of thyme
50g/2 oz (½ stick) butter
salt and black pepper
100ml/3½ fl oz (½ cup) vegetable stock

Corona
50g/2 oz (½ stick) butter
1 carrot, 1 celery stick and 1 onion, finely chopped
350g/12 oz (2 cups) Carnaroli rice (or Vialone nano or Arborio)
1 litre/1¾ pints (4 cups) vegetable stock
salt and black pepper
50g/2 oz (generous ½ cup) freshly grated Parmesan

Preheat the oven to 180°C/350°F. Lightly grease a ring mold, then pre-pare the vegetables for the center. Melt the butter in a pan and stir in the vegetables, thyme and seasoning. Cook for 5 minutes then add the stock, bring to a boil, cover and simmer for 10 minutes. Remove from the heat and keep warm.

To make the rice *Corona*, melt half the butter and cook the carrot, celery and onion until soft. Add the rice and stir around the pan for 5 minutes, then start adding the stock, a ladle at a time. Continue stirring for 15 minutes then add the remaining butter, seasoning and Parmesan.

Spoon the rice mixture into the ring mold, levelling down the top. Bake for 20 minutes. Remove from the oven and leave to stand for 5 minutes. Cover with a serving plate and invert to turn out. Drain the vegetables and arrange in the center, serving any left over separately.

Soufflé di Riso all'Arancio

Rice and Orange Soufflé

Although rice is used in many Italian desserts the results are often not very exciting. This soufflé has an interesting texture and the almond and orange flavor is a favorite Mediterranean taste introduced by the Arabs centuries ago.

Serves 4

500ml/18 fl oz (2 cups) milk
80g/3 oz caster or granulated sugar
50g/2 oz (½ stick) butter
zest of 1 orange
150g/5½ oz (1 scant cup) Vialone nano rice
(or Carnaroli or Arborio)
4 eggs, separated
80g/3 oz blanched almonds, chopped
80g/3 oz candied orange peel, diced
100ml/3½ fl oz (½ cup) orange liqueur

Preheat the oven to 220°C/425°F and butter a large soufflé dish.

In a heavy-bottomed pan, bring the milk to a boil with half the sugar, butter and orange zest. Stir in the rice and cook slowly, stirring frequently. I usually put a heat diffuser under the pan. When cooked turn into a mixing bowl and allow to cool. This part of the recipe can be prepared in advance. Stir in the egg yolks, remaining sugar, almonds, orange peel and liqueur. Beat the egg whites until stiff then fold into the mixture. Turn into the soufflé dish and bake for about 35 minutes until well risen and firm to the touch.

MINESTRA DI SCORFANO

Scorpion Fish Minestra

The *scorfano*, known in French as *rascasse*, is a red fish with unpleasant needle-sharp bones and a large head. The Italians have an expression 'ugly as a scorfano'. Ugly it may be but it has a superb flavor, and is a vital ingredient in all the great Mediterranean fish soups. You can substitute any good, strong flavored fish. It seems a miracle that one small fish can make such a good starter for four people, and it is even more of a miracle that there is no oil or butter in the recipe!

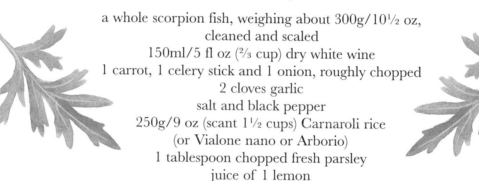

SERVES 4

a whole scorpion fish, weighing about 300g/10½ oz,
cleaned and scaled
150ml/5 fl oz (⅔ cup) dry white wine
1 carrot, 1 celery stick and 1 onion, roughly chopped
2 cloves garlic
salt and black pepper
250g/9 oz (scant 1½ cups) Carnaroli rice
(or Vialone nano or Arborio)
1 tablespoon chopped fresh parsley
juice of 1 lemon

Put the fish in a large pan with 500ml/18 fl oz (2 cups) cold, lightly salted water, the wine, the roughly chopped vegetables and peeled garlic cloves. Bring to a boil, cover and simmer for 15 minutes. Remove from the heat and, when it is cool, carefully remove the fish and place in a covered bowl in the fridge. Place the vegetables and cooking liquid in another bowl in the fridge to form a jelly as it chills.

To make the *minestra*, remove the fish from the bone, taking care to pick out all the small bones, and reserve. Blend or process the vegetables in the jelly and return to the pan with another 500ml/18 fl oz (2 cups) of water. Check the seasoning and bring back to a boil. Pour in the rice and simmer for 15 to 20 minutes until cooked, then add the large flakes of fish with the parsley and lemon juice and serve.

RISOTTO CON OSTRICHE E CHAMPAGNE

≈≈

Risotto with Oysters and Champagne

The young German chef, Heinz Beck, serves this dish at 'La Pergola' restaurant in Rome. You need to ask a fishmonger to teach you how to open oysters if you want to preserve and use their liquid.

SERVES 4

20 oysters in their shells
4 tablespoons arugula, shredded
2 red tomatoes, peeled, deseeded (see page 25) and finely chopped
200ml/7 fl oz (1 cup) champagne
2 tablespoons extra virgin olive oil
350g/12 oz (2 cups) Carnaroli rice (or Vialone nano or Arborio)
1 litre/1¾ pints (4 cups) light meat or fish stock
salt and black pepper

Remove the oysters from their shells and place them in a bowl with their liquid, the arugula, tomatoes and half the champagne.

Heat the oil in a large pan, add the rice and stir for 5 minutes. Stir in the remaining champagne and then gradually start adding the stock a little at a time as it is absorbed by the rice. When the rice is cooked but still *al dente*, after about 15 to 20 minutes, remove from the heat and stir in the oyster mixture. Adjust the seasoning and serve with more champagne!

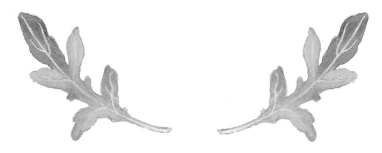

Risotto all'Aragosta

≈≈

Lobster Risotto

An opulent risotto served on very special occasions.

Serves 4

200ml/7 fl oz (1 cup) dry white wine
1 carrot and 1 leek, roughly chopped
4 peppercorns
1 small lobster
3 tablespoons extra virgin olive oil
1 onion, finely sliced
300g/10½ oz (1⅔ cups) Carnaroli rice
(or Vialone nano or Arborio)
4 tablespoons fresh tomato sauce (see page 15)
1 tablespoon finely chopped fresh parsley
salt and black pepper
2 teaspoons lemon juice

Bring 1.5 litres/2¾ pints (6 cups) lightly salted water to a boil. Put in half the wine with the carrot, leek and peppercorns and boil for 15 minutes. Add the lobster and boil for another 15 minutes. Strain the cooking liquid and reserve and allow the lobster to cool before removing the shell. Crush the claws, remove all the flesh and chop. Slice the tail into rounds and keep to one side.

Heat half the oil in a large pan and gently fry the onion until soft. Stir in the rice and after 5 minutes stir in the remaining wine with the tomato sauce. Pour in the reserved lobster stock a little at a time and keep stirring, adding more when it has been absorbed. After 15 to 20 minutes, the rice will be cooked. Remove from the heat, stir in the chopped lobster and half the parsley and check the seasoning. Heat the remaining oil and lightly fry the slices of lobster tail with the rest of the parsley. Serve over the top of the risotto and sprinkle lemon juice over the lobster flesh.

INDEX

ACKNOWLEDGEMENTS

I would like to thank MAUREEN GREEN in London and PHIL ALLEN in Rome who gave me words of encouragement before I started this book, and HEATHER HOLDEN-BROWN and JO ROBERTS-MILLER at Headline for their warmth and enthusiasm. I would also like to thank SARAH HOCOMBE whose illustrations are always full of color and life.

In Italy in my researching and eating I owe thanks to: AIMO and NADIA MORONI from Aimo e Nadia restaurant, Milan; DANIA LUCHERINI from La Chiusa restaurant, Montefollonico; THE GUERRA FAMILY at Il Melograno hotel, Monopoli; MAURIZIO MARTIN at Osteria Da Fiore, Venice; FULVIO PIERANGELINI at Gambero Rosso, San Vincenzo; Ristorante Il Paiolo, Vercelli; Cascina dei Fiori, Borgo Vercelli; SILVERIO CINERI, Ristorante Silverio, Bologna; CLAUDIA and TONINO VERRO, La Contea, Neive; LIVIA and ALFONSO IACCARINO, Don Alfonso, Sant'Agata sui due Golfi; HEINZ BECK, La Pergola, Rome; Ristorante Cocchi, Parma.

Among the rice producers in Italy I would like to thank: Dr GUIDO GUARDIGLI from Cascina Veneria; FULVIO FONTE from Azienda Agricola Lodigiana; GABRIELE FERRON from Riseria Ferron; Riso Gallo. They helped me with my research, and their superb quality rice helped me to cook some memorable dishes.